ROCKED
by the
WATERS

ROCKED
by the
WATERS

Poems of Motherhood

Margaret Hasse & Athena Kildegaard

Editors

NODIN PRESS

ISBN: 978-21-947237-26-1

Library of Congress Control Number: 2020932870
Cover photograph credit: GIST: Yarn & Fiber
Design: John Toren

The editors wish to thank Norton Stillman for believing in this project; John Toren for making it beautiful; and Stewart Lindstrom and Trina Vue, Morris Academic Partners, the University of Minnesota Morris, for their dedication to details.

Nodin Press, LLC
5114 Cedar Lake Road
Minneapolis, MN
55416

www.nodinpress.com

Printed in USA

to everyone rocked by the waters

CONTENTS

TELL ME OF THIS PARTING

ALL THE WORDS BY HEART

INTRODUCTION

We were poets long before we became mothers, Athena through birth and Margaret through adoption. And then we learned, like so many mother poets before us, how to weave a writing life and a mothering life together. Margaret found a foremother of the motherhood poem in Sylvia Plath and Athena in Sharon Olds. Our mothering entered our poems. We found ourselves concerned for the environment and for racial injustice because we had very dear skin in the game of the future.

Our lives as mothers and poets mirror a shift in poems of motherhood observed by The Poetry Foundation in its introduction to a recent online collection called "Poems of Motherhood": "Poems that represented the real, lived experiences of mothers remained hard to find until the 1970s, the time of the second-wave feminist movement." Before that time, poems about motherhood weren't considered appropriate for publication in literary journals, or they were mawkish glorifications of mothers that appeared in "ladies' magazines." Plath and Olds, our outspoken literary forebears, made a channel for more mother poets to write authentically about motherhood, and over the half century since, that channel has widened and deepened. Mother poets are writing about more aspects of motherhood in new ways and their work is being taken seriously. Turn to almost any literary publication today and you'll find a poem about motherhood.

Although there have been several excellent anthologies of poems about motherhood in recent years, the time was ripe for another. The subject of motherhood is so vast, we mother poets are not finished writing about it, and so there is an abundance of poems worth reading.

Furthermore, at our southern border, the government separates mothers—and fathers, too—from their children. Legislation is being passed in many states that reduces women's autonomy over our bodies and choices about motherhood. In many parts of our country, prenatal care and daycare are inadequate. In an environment in which motherhood is threatened, we need poems that look squarely at the "real, lived experiences" of mothers.

We began our process of shaping this anthology by looking around at the work of mother poets. We first shared with one another poems by living American poets whose work we admired. This small cache of poems helped us frame for ourselves what we desired in an anthology: music, surprise, experiment, tradition, variety, and also joy and despair and grace.

Lacking the administrative wherewithal to manage the deluge that might come to us through an open call for poems, having little experience in compiling an anthology, living 200 miles apart, and being Minnesotans with a deep love of our state and its literary community, we began by inviting mother poets in Minnesota to send us poems. From that dip into the waters, we reached out around the country. With each cast of our net, we asked poets to recommend other living mother poets. Then on a glistening weekend at Margaret's cabin near Nisswa, we read aloud to one another all the poems received. We laughed and cried and rejoiced in the voices who joined us in that small space. What a pleasure to be together, reading to each other things that delighted and inspirited us—work that felt deeply inevitable and right in the way that good poems do.

As we began selecting and ordering poems, we saw lacunae in the gathering, and so we found poems to fill some of the spaces, though there remain absences. Let there be more poems and anthologies of motherhood! This anthology draws together inspired and diverse voices of living American women exploring motherhood's rich complexities. These poems examine the consciousness of writers newly become mothers and the changed consciousness when their lives and the lives of their children change and when the world around us changes.

We hope that this anthology, like a good gift, is both a comfort and a source of amazement. Here are familiar poets and new poets and noted writers new to poetry—poets we're honored to introduce to a larger audience. Some of these poems sneak up to motherhood and others address motherhood from the first line. Meet a mother who spars with her children using outrageous names with good humor, and another who reminds us of how much bounce we gave our babies. In some poems, mothers watch their children learn their first words, go off to college, or make their own decisions (and mistakes). In others, mothers wrestle with the heartache of children who struggle, are estranged, or have died too soon. The poems are written by new mothers and by mothers with grandchildren, single mothers, queer mothers, and even a mother-daughter pair. Here are serious and funny, short and epic, intimate and political poems, poems in free lyric form, and also prose poems, a sonnet, and one etheree.

The phrase that became our title for this anthology is from Katharine Rauk's poem "Casida of the Weeping." *Rocked by the Waters* captures the sense of motherhood as being always in flux. *Rocked* reminds us of cradles and carseats and our own arms bearing children through the day and night. It reminds us also of the give and take—the rocking—required to nurture children into puberty and beyond. And it recalls large changes, upheavals, and astonishment. *Water* conjures associations of babies floating in amniotic fluid and requiring milk to survive; mothers weeping and drying children's tears; the gulfs that open between mothers and children and the ways we cross those gulfs; the great metaphorical water table of mothers being in community together. We were surprised, and then not, by how often images of water appear in these poems.

We were surprised, too, by the myriad images of the night sky these mother poets have drawn on. And then we realized that, of course, the moon and her phases and tides are ours and have been for centuries. There's no hysteria in these poems—there is, we learned, an embrace of motherhood as earthy and universal.

Rather than a chronology of stages of motherhood as the anthology's organizing principle, we drew on the images of water and sky to hold together the poems in thematic groups. We hope you'll have as much pleasure as we did discovering the many ways these poems are in conversation with one another. Yes, this was a labor of love, born of our own delights and upheavals, conceived to widen the way for more poems of motherhood.

Margaret Hasse & Athena Kildegaard, Editors
January 2020

FOREWORD

When I was studying creative writing, I often received one of two reactions to the poetry I was writing: disdain or celebration, and always for the same reason. I was writing my way through (in)fertility and swollen pregnancy. Any words I threw at these disembodied embodied experiences were both alienating and liberating for both myself and my peers. How can these poems so very much be two things at once?

In one of my final meetings with one of my advisors, I was told, in a kind of conspiratorial way, "You know, your audience is incredibly narrow for this work." I was early mother-tired, damp with new-milk, and remember saying something like, "That's not why I'm writing these poems," with a metaphorical toss of my head, and didn't press the matter anymore. At that point, I was ready to be done, to fold my poems into a perfect bound book, gold-stamped, and graduate.

That was eight years ago. My daughter was born during the final year of the writing program, and now she's long and lean and still embodies every person I write my poems to and for. I wouldn't be so glib if I were asked the question about audience again.

The problem is that writers and readers are told that poems about motherhood are hard to identify with. They are too narrow in sphere, don't belong amongst the more ambitious poems that go beyond the domestic. Perhaps this is true, to a degree. But, to me, this might be a complaint applied to any poem that is "about" one single other thing. We write our human lives through war and cancer and make metaphors of them both. We write our ways through the alarm of the climate crisis and the landscapes of our homes. We write into and out of our experiences and our sense of wonder because it is what we are drawn to do. The risk of the mother-poem is that it turns away a reader's head too quickly with assumptions; it is believed to be too sentimental, too trite, before it is given a chance to be itself.

For me, a poem about any phase of motherness is about everything, for in motherhood we envelop all the energy of any emotion we've felt up until now: hope and fear and clarity and disillusion and exhaustion and desire and guilt and hunger. As Carolyn Williams-Noren writes in "Writing About the First Months," one of her poems in this anthology, "No adjective changes baby." No noun encapsulates motherhood.

The same might be said for any experience that transforms us utterly. The days my children were born changed all days before and after—the world was rent in two. I am midway through my life, I hope, which means there will be other renderings—losses and moves and decisions we make (or that make us) that leave us forever one thing different from what we were months before. But surely the readers who look down on the pages of a mother-poem have had those experiences too—the renderings—and can see that this is one of the lenses through which we see the world?

Perhaps it's because the motherhood story is the one that is wholly familiar and completely unique that allows it to be two things at once. Or that when we become mothers, we must *be* two things at once—when my daughter was born, my attention learned to be forever divided.

These eight years, I've learned our bodies can become, as Arielle Goldberg calls it in "Honey," "a menagerie for bright orange creatures." I've read and celebrated unique stories of motherhood: Jenn Givhan's memory of "the hotel basin I first / bathed him in, waiting for adoption papers / in an unfamiliar city" ("Jeremiah Growing") and Rachel Moritz's "gloved trainer of chromosome, / spun in a bucket / from the well drawn up, / my own face inside" ("Kairos (Conception)"). What glories these pieces can be!

Poems of motherhood demand not only an examination of how we exist in relation to the world, but also how we give the world to our children. Layli Long Soldier, in "Whereas Statement [13]," writes:

WHEREAS her birth signaled the responsibility as mother
to teach what it is to be Lakota, therein the question: what
did I know about being Lakota? Signaled panic, blood rush

my embarrassment. What did I know of our language but pieces?

In her poem "Mother daughter hour," Camille T. Dungy's sense of language and juxtaposition is also acute: "Callie is reading the book about language, / and I am reading the book about death."

In poems of motherhood, readers can experience broader perspectives, opening up the world. We are well beyond the door of the domestic. In Ellen Bass's words,

> For a moment
> it seems possible that every frailty, every pain,
> could be an opening, a crack that lets the unexpected
> reach us.

Every poem in this collection is a miracle—every experience with depth and validity a work of art.

I was pregnant with my son when I was a fellow in The Loft Literary Center's mentorship program. His first days on this planet were spent being passed around a table of men and women who have gone on to publish first and second books, to be visiting writers in esteemed programs, and to found prison writing workshops. Their literary voices have saved my life, over and over. I can only hope some of these voices do the same for you.

Molly Sutton Kiefer
Publisher of Tinderbox Editions & Poet / Essayist
January 2020

MOTHERING

Freya Manfred

Mothering was born
in the salty womb that shaped us
when the first wave met land,
crashing from the past into the future—

and a membrane grew a heart and two swallowing eyes,
and vessels carried first blood,
and our hands tended, touched, cradled, and rocked,
just as we were rocked in that ancient water—

so that those who come from us, all surprised,
can circle, sigh, cry, and create more of us,
the most natural motion in the world:
to reach beyond ourselves, and protect that reaching out.

We mothers are the first circle
within the circle of the earth,
within the solar system, within the Milky Way,
within the universe—

which is a long and round and endless road.

Show Us How to See You

PRAISE POEM FOR MY SON (SUN) NICHOLAS ON HIS 13TH BIRTHDAY

JP Howard

praise you, son of two mamas.
praise all the joy you bring to this world.
praise you brilliant beam of light.
praise you bird-watcher. poet. lover of math and science. builder of
robots. artist. gentle soul.
sometimes so serious and sometimes so silly.
praise your curly fro. stay curious and aware.
praise your powerful voice. praise that poem you wrote at age seven,
wishing that Trayvon's parents could hear his voice "just one more time."
praise the lens through which you see the world, honest and unflinching.
praise all the black boys who live to tell their stories.
praise how you love nature. praise those photos you take.
praise your paintings and your sketches.
praise how you document the world around you.
praise your two mamas.
praise your big brother.
praise how you celebrate our queer family.
praise chosen families and the paths we walk each day.
praise all the poems i wrote and will keep writing for you and your brother.
praise how y'all fill my pages and my heart.
praise your teen talkback.
praise how your mamas give you space to grow into your best self.
praise mistakes you will make and lessons to be learned.
praise your lean body growing growing growing towards manhood.
praise all this love that fills my heart when I think of you shining sun.
son, keep being your best most brilliant self.

HOLDING HER

Kathryn Kysar

In the twilight of the evening,
as the last beads of light slip through
green velvet curtains that hang like moss,
her ten month old body
curls itself around my middle,
her face buried in my breast,
her silken skin freshly bathed,
her limbs curved and heavy with sleep.
  The world holds still;
the earth stops on its axis
and hangs, complete in this pause,
the sky and moon silenced
by the breath of a sleeping babe.

Helium Dream

Sanjana Nair

for A.

Oxygen

Your body is built of my body:
Blood, 0.006% iron, give or take.
The metal never lets the oxygen down,
though I will and you will
name it and I am already gray
wanting warmth beside your fire.
We are still made of dust.

Phosphorous

If I might say as much about color
as you—naming skin blonde,
the way tan is just tan for you.
When you find Polaroids of me
will you name my color out of the spectrum
of science? The fading colors left behind.
By then, I will be dust.

Carbon

I love the bones of my wrists
when they balance you, when they touch
the sharp edge of your cheekbone.
This gaze: Never will I love myself the way I love you,
Girl, Unspoiled. I won't let them talk to you about—
Don't ever let them say that—
Some were born with dust in their eyes.

Hydrogen

Non-toxic, odorless, childproof, safe:
If untouched. I wish no ill hands to find you,
or combust the body of you.

How you will burst into your 20's,
and how I will shade my eyes. I know.
I've stared at the sun too long, broken over the fact
that stars burn so bright long after they turn dust.

Sulfur

I break into the smooth, white-bone color,
the just-solid, five-minute gold of the perfect egg:
Sustenance. You watch. And I watch you:
The awe of what is to be consumed,
the terror of its origins, the life cut short.
Little girl, let your unspoiled splendid crash
into my arms. Make dust of fear and remain.

Nitrogen

Atomic number 7, fertilizer of my dreams.
Be a spore and land, become the woman before
and let there be a woman after.
The key, born while I was out gazing at stars. My mother
sang this song, and so will you: Stay
beside me, place your hand in mine. Forget the chains
have burned, will burn: You will commit them to dust.

PINE

Ye Chun

When your red limbs unfold like petals,
my needles are falling.

When your soles are snail chill,
my needles are falling.

My brown-haired child, I've seen you
walk toward me bare-footed,

dreaming to be known.
I've seen you lie down on my golden needles

to be framed by your own stillness.
I say breathe, my child, breathe.

I've heard your red heartbeats,
red hoofs leaping.

His Thirteenth Spring

Tracy Youngblom

This is the child who once asked me
        where heaven is, not
approximately but precisely: above us
        or intermingled with
the vaporous clouds or some other
        named place? He bends
down to talk now, avoids my eyes,
        wearing those heavy
shoes he needed, wondering if I want
        to play tennis
on the driveway, since it's not yet
        dark.

Sky reaches down, blue circle burning
        indigo, released heat
rising around our wet feet. Birds flare
        from tree to bush,
become shadow and hum as we lob
        the ball back
and forth. It arcs in brief illumination
        toward our hidden faces.
I'm pretty bad at this, I say. *You just need
        a little encouragement,*
he says. Our echoing steps. *Here it is,*
        he says, *here.*

For W.

Joanna Solfrian

My difficult one, I love you for your difficulties,
the door that closes on your thumb, the strap that's too tight,
the root vegetable that retains too much rootiness.

Oceans rise in me when I watch your curled form sleep.
When you answer a stranger's question, you are a tamer
of inner lions. You release others' laughter the way

a conductor releases a tuba's belch.
I love how you stomp your foot at injustice
and then become sorrowful for your foot,

which you console with the salt of your tears.
All your premonitions will come true, which is why
I am grateful your intoxicating scent has thorns.

When I sing lullabies into your shell ears, the ocean
sings back, and you exhale dreams into the inch of air
between us. And when I cry, it is you who pats my back.

THE SCOOTERS

Leslie Adrienne Miller

Summer mornings at eight they clatter
over the seams in the sidewalks, boys
hurtling downhill, one foot riding,
and one tucked behind. They could all
tell you how many joints rend
the slab from block end to block end,
and which ones jolt all the way
to the sternum. Their fleet cries
ring like chains, whatever words
they leave on the air reduced to trill
and plea. Among them my spawn
on his yard sale Razor, learning
the supremacy of speed and noise.
They all have bikes on which
they can command more rush
and silence, but the din
of I'm here-ness, the racket
of see me, see me, see me
is refrain to the bright sear
of breakage ripping through
half the families on the block.
One towhead peels on gravel
at the alley turn, rakes his knees
in puddle sludge and grit; another
leads him limping to a mother,
any mother now that the message
has gotten through: we're interchange-
able, standing at all the back doors
armed with antiseptic and soap,
trying to ward off loss of limb,
learning to bow to dominion's
noisy grief, to know the difference
between the yowl of a surface scrape
and the keen of a lasting wound.

Now She Can Crawl

Alice Duggan

Oh the brisk swish of her hips—she
has places to go, you can't know
how the stairs call her name,
or the dark inside she's
going to find
over there.

AREN, TWO YEARS OLD, PLAYING AT ORCHARD PARK

Kris Bigalk

When the other mothers' eyes leave their own children,
stare at him, then at me, when their small talk
carefully circles the questions they want to ask:
What is wrong with him? How did it happen?

I want to tell them how, when he was one day old,
he stopped mid-breath, lips bluing.
I touched his cheeks, puffing air against
his sweet-bowed mouth until he
sighed against my ear, until his dusky
skin turned pink again, and he agreed
to stay, but not wholly.

I want to tell them how I held
hopes, at first flickering like fireflies,
in my cupped hands, a glance
of light glinting now and then
between my fingers,
but when I opened
my palms, their gray bodies
curled up like withered prayers,
dry as paper.

I want to tell them how I wait
for the cool May nights to come this year,
how I will take him out into the
dew-flecked grass, the little sea-glass green lights
of fireflies glittering around our feet and knees,
how this time, I will catch my prayers
delicately, only for a moment, then release
them back to the lilac scented, cricket song night,
how I will teach him to do the same.

ETHEREE FOR MY SUNS/SONS IN AMERIKA

JP Howard

no joke, raising black sons in this country
no matter how bright they shine, they black
sometimes their blackness closes doors
or screams *no justice, no peace!*
and no racist police!
i rock them to sleep,
their black, night sky
filled with stars,
shining
suns

sons
can hear
me humming
them lullabies
in their dreams, i think
i can hear them chanting
mama, please stop worrying
they don't know, when they are so still
i still lean in close, listen for breath
whisper, sons your black is so beautiful

FRACTALS

Julie Gard

Don't touch me, my daughter says half the time I reach out. The other half she takes my hand, leans into me. The other half of the time, she's the one reaching for me. When she says don't touch me, half of the time she's already sitting next to me with her left side pressed against my right. Half of the time, she is across the room and I'm reading a book. She wants to know if it's a book about her. Then she's angry, if it is or if it's not.

Summons

Catherine Barnett

Do I have a Certificate of Good Conduct,
Justice Milton Tingling wants to know.

I don't think I do, no—
For years I asked the court for exemptions

and when I did serve I was useless,
I didn't care about the chiropractor and his wife,

about theft, delinquency, malfeasance.
Justice was a beautiful

abstraction I counted on from within the walls
of my exhausted mothermind.

It's a long time since I've been summoned,
and now Milton Tingling

has replaced County Clerk Norman Goodman,
who ruled the courts for forty-five years,

including the eighteen it took me to raise my son.
You don't know me, Justice Tingling,

but I like the sound of your name,
I like the sound of Justice Anything,

you who refuse to honor exemptions
I have none of now.

The boy is no longer exempt, no,
and I want to serve, I want to make amends

for my absences,
my failures of civic duty.

I don't need to ask for time to raise him,
he's been raised, he no longer lives with me,

he's not waiting for me to come pick him up
to the sound of twenty questions

and the sound of the phone ringing and the dead dog barking.
He's a mystery to me,

old enough now for his own summons,
Justice Tingling, but he's not home

to receive it or fill it out,
he's not here to answer your questionnaire

about his own Good Conduct.
I listen to the traffic outside my window,

what would I do without it, it's a boon,
it croons,

it idled us through the days I tended
to the child who right at this moment

might be drinking his own lovely self
into a stupor

or watching the fraternity kids
drink themselves into stupors

in the basement and backrooms
of a self-replicating Upsilon Upsilon

across whose exterior in black poster paint
early one spring morning

someone spray-painted the words *rape haven*.
Anonymous, the papers said.

Anonymous, the brothers said
for the brother who is not my son, no,

my son has no brothers, Justice Tingling,
he's an only child, or he's only

a man now
who for all I know is or is not,

is or is not
with other young men

washing paint off a stone wall
with a high-powered hose and a stiff brush

like it never happened,
like it never happens.

Justice, forgive me.
Forgive me, Justice.

Field Trip

Pamela Schmid

The day we netted a tadpole
from leaf brack and learned that frogs
soak up the world's tears,
you fashioned a dragonfly
from a coffee filter and magic
marker; twice folded, dipped in water,
it purpled and blued as mud still clung
to our soles and we waited for colors
to bleed upward, like tie-dyed stars.
When you asked me to twist on the pipe
cleaner antennae, I obeyed—even though
I thought *we could start something here,*
thought *you can, not me*—but I
wanted to see this one thing through.
This was the week we sold the only
house you ever knew, the week
before those four letters—A-D-H-D—
would arrive on crisp white paper
and lock in the puzzle's last piece.
Brain fog sinks ships and I sing
to keep you near. My froglet, I can see
how the stubs at your side have sturdied
into legs, the apoptosis of your fine
unnecessary tail, how Pisces floats
inside you—celestial seabreath—
starpoints too slick to grasp.

CELLS ALL RINGING

Lesley Wheeler

It was not the sick shudder of a small plane, windshield
scratched, scenery blurred, or the snarl of a finger sliding
beneath an envelope flap. It was more like waking up
after a doze on a plastic raft, noticing the shore is far off
and the sky plum—not terrifying yet, just enough time
to paddle in, pack up blankets and slowly rusting chairs,
children who are no longer small. Or it was like not
hearing a toddler babble about toy sharks beyond
a half-closed door, realizing you've been not hearing her
for a few minutes now. She suddenly became fourteen
and it's dinner and she's describing the pregnant girl in Earth
Science as she doesn't eat her page of cod, scribbled with herbs
and strips of wine-poached pepper. *I sort of admire
her,* she says. *She's getting really fat now.* You correct her,
unwarily: *Not fat. A seven-month-belly is hard and full
of baby.* And then rising tones behind her fully-closed
door. Daughter and friend emerge to ask, *How far along
until you start to show?* It turns out to be another
teenager, not your sensible girl whose slender left hip buzzes
with texts until stars vibrate in a perfectly
dry night sky like messages, like fish in deep
water or the unnecessarily frightened passengers
on a small plane about to land. A shell's secretive
murmur reminds you of the sea but is really your own
blood echoing through nearby coils. Sound reflected,
not by a mirror. By the whorls of your daughter,
loaded with mysterious cargo and about to launch.

LOVE LIKE HORSES

Athena Kildegaard

for my daughter

And when you wrote me a note—
you were not even in school yet—
to say you loved me more than horses,
though you'd never spent even an hour
in the company of a horse, I could not
imagine how you could have formed
this abstract love, this, when you were
too small to look into a mirror unless
I held you up; and when you came to me
when I was chopping peppers and celery,
years later, though not so much later that you'd
left home, and you leaned toward me across
our kitchen island and asked, forthrightly
because that was the way you'd learned
to find out what you needed to know—
you asked me what an orgasm was like—
it was then, looking at you as if
for the first time again, a sharp knife
in my hand, the crisp celestial scent
of celery rising from the chopping block,
it was then that I felt again the bliss
of giving your cantering body to another,
of opening completely, of letting
your beautiful body run full out.

Imagined (Overlong) Text Message to My Daughter Who Is Studying in Turkey

Lia Rivamonte

You say it's hot in Tarsus, blistering
even in the shade of the café awning where
you and your new friend Çinar sip
banana milk in a bath of sulk and sweat
on the sidewalk of that teeming city.

That city on the Cilician plains near
the mouth of the cay where Zeus flung
his faithful Pegasus out into the deepest
reaches of the night and the winged
horse's body fragmented

into radiant bits—a portrait in stars
for eternity; and where a single feather
from the wing of the beast floated
softly down to earth to rest atop
the rubble and dust but is now buried

beneath still-gleaming bronzes poured
by artful Hittites to decorate their fiercest
warriors felled by the Assyrians swallowed
up by the Persian Empire that surrendered
to the Romans who were overtaken

by the Muslims who, in turn, were defeated
by Byzantine Heraclius who lost to the Seljuk Turks,
who then were foiled by the Ottoman Turks. And where,
some enchanted evening long, long ago the queenly
Cleo and bodacious Mark A. locked eyes igniting

a flame so hot even the most complacent gods fell
to their knees melting with lust, and where

that pair, glutted with love and ambition feasted
in carnal impunity and built their ill-fated fleet;
And where Saul was born and raised

a Jew, and who, on routine business
to Damascus, was smote
by a violent, inexplicable light then reborn
Paul, the saint for whom the city
in which you were born was named.

Please, dear girl, tell me you have seen
the severed arm of the mummy, stood
in the shadow of Cleopatra's Gate, studied
the Tomb of the Seven Sleepers and
sampled the şalgam and çezerye.

This city, this Tarsus, is part of you now—
your story—temporarily documented
by the pictures you posted last Tuesday
on your Insta. BTW, your new friend looks
nice—who is he, exactly?

Whirling

Julie Landsman

Flat black hat on his head, long beard,
the rabbi dances in circles.
Faster and faster he twirls the circle of men,
her son among them, clapping and chanting
around the tables mounded with purple flowers,
and lettuce blossoms in deep maroon
piled on small gold plates. She remembers,
how years ago, he went to the Sangre De Cristo Mountains,
to stay in the wilderness with Sufi dancers.
He wrote her a postcard: "Whirl from sunrise to sunset
on the purple mesa." Now, she wants to break in
on the dance as she wanted to break into the loneliness
of her son's dervish time. Spiraling black suits
do not allow her velvet into their candled dance.
So, she watches. When it is over, he rests a few tables away,
his arm stretches along the back of his wife's chair,
his hand cups the skin of her shoulder.
He glances across the room, lifts his eyes over the flowers,
over the heads of his cousins; waves and smiles at her.
For a moment she is in his circle, has come to rest
within his life, the dancing done.

To One Now Grown

Naomi Shihab Nye

If we could start over, I would let you get dirtier.
Place your face in the food, it's okay.

In trade for great metaphors,
the ones you used to spout every minute,
I'd extend your bedtime,
be more patient with tantrums,
never answer urgency with urgency,
try to stay serene.

In one scene you are screaming
and I stop the car.
What do we do next?
I can't remember.
It's buried in the drawer of small socks.

Give me the box of time.
Let's make it bigger.
It's all yours.

The Boy I Quit For

Deborah Keenan

He's lovely, handsome, really.
When he arrived he had sunlight
White hair, rococo curls, gray/blue
Eyes oceanic and peering.

Now his hair's dark, straight, he's
Slender as reeds, slender as a mirror.
And smells of dense tobacco, of
Cigarette packs and ashtrays
From Toronto and Biscayne Bay.

When he arrived before dawn,
Serious and ours, I resolved to
Stop smoking—no other choice,
Really, with his skin smelling
Of angel and hair, of soap and
Pure white cotton towels—no way
To keep the vice that kept me slim
And gave me such filtered pleasure.

Then I started again, not til he was
Two or so, then finally stopped, and
Sent him a letter. Dear J. I wrote,
You're the boy I quit for in honor
Of life and love, wisdom and will power.
I quit for you, because it's right
That I should. I suffered the required
Length of time, and moved on, and
He moved on, moved out, and he's
Lovely, handsome, really, with
Gray/blue eyes and he moves
With grace through smoke
And I can see him clearly though
I can barely see him.

Abeyance

Rebecca Foust

letter to my transgender daughter

I made soup tonight, with cabbage, chard
and thyme picked outside our back door.
For this moment the room is warm and light,
and I can presume you safe somewhere.
I know the night lives inside you. I know grave,
sad errors were made, dividing you, and hiding
you from you inside. I know a girl like you
was knifed last week, another set aflame.
I know I lack the words, or all the words I say
are wrong. I know I'll call and you won't answer,
and still I'll call. I want to tell you
you were loved with all I had, recklessly,
and with abandon, loved the way the cabbage
in my garden near-inverts itself, splayed
to catch each last ray of sun. And how
the feeling furling-in only makes the heart
more dense and green. Tonight it seems like
something one could bear.

Guess what, Dad and I finally figured out Pandora,
and after all those years of silence, our old music
fills the air. It fills the air, and somehow, here,
at this instance and for this instant only
—perhaps three bars—what I recall
equals all I feel, and I remember all the words.

My daughter, My hero

Jessi Marie Faue

I will not tell my daughter
How my childhood left me afraid, at night
Lying in bed tucking my patchwork quilt around my small body
Making believe that it would protect me from
An older brother's sexual desires.

I will not tell my daughter
How I was ignored for being curious,
Hurt for asking too many questions, punished by
Being locked in a basement for hours. Forgotten in the cold
Northern Michigan darkness.

I will not tell my daughter
About my sadness to have a biological mother
Who had addictions stronger than her ability
To care for my sister and me
Or that being adopted didn't mean becoming
Part of a loving family.

I will not tell my daughter
How joining the Army was a means to get away, but
Being in the Army was both a blessing and a curse
An opportunity to be seen while
Trying to stay hidden behind the camouflage.

I will not tell my daughter how
Terrified I was of becoming her mother
Worried of making similar mistakes,
Staying awake at night, reading every parenting book
Rubbing my growing belly
Praying I would get it right.

I will not tell my daughter these things,
These things that left me feeling broken inside.
I will not tell her
Until the time is right.

Until then, I will tell her
I love you every chance I can.

I will tell my daughter
How I hope she grows to have her mother's resilience
To overcome the parts of life that are hard,
While embracing and accepting the good.

I will tell my daughter
How I kissed her tiny face above
The bridge of her nose because
My lips fit perfectly in that space
I will tell her
How I sang "Wagon Wheel" and "You Are My Sunshine"
To lull her to sleep.

I will tell my daughter
That my heart grew when she was born.
For the first time, I felt a love so deep that I knew
We would be okay.

I will tell my daughter
That I will fight for her without question,
That the world is hers to explore,
That she should never settle for anything
Less than she deserves
Because she is worthy.

I will tell my daughter
That she is smart, brave, and full of wonder.
I will tell her
That she has taught me how to be a mother.
Being a mother has taught me about love
And together, it is helping to make me whole.

I will tell her how she saved my life.

Yes

Emilie Buchwald

These questions you ask me
with your eyes

I would answer yes
to you always
yes   yes   yes

I would sugar your strawberries
with my yes

I would pack yes
into your lunches with the cookies,
crack and peel the hardest days,
and wrap them in the foil
of my shielding yes

At night
I imagine
feeling my way
to your stabled bodies
and finding that
you have moved
out of the house
out of the yard,
into spaces
I can't share.

I promise you
a waking passport
out of the country of casual knives
that slash because you are
too small   too tall   too blue   too red.

I promise you
something better than a promise.

You will grow
out of clothes too tight for you,
the garments of smaller persuasions.

You will grow
to imagine
yourselves.

You will grow
up out of the leaf
out of the shadow
of my yes.

The Heart Becomes an Ocean

SKINNY DIPPING WHILE PREGNANT

Amy Young

Stars tell stories
upside down.

The lake spills
into night, the dock

a backbone shifting
underfoot.

A dip of toe
crinkles the moon. I walk

on the moon barefoot, blind
where knees meet water,

the fish curious,
who pucker

hard lips
against my shins.

Belly taut, I dive
into anise sky. I turn

somersaults. Tides
rush through me.

Pulled by a different
weight, I am

my own galaxy.

ON CONTAINING MULTITUDES:

Zoë Ryder White

For three weeks, I had three knots
of cells in me. They gamboled around
in the dark, eating everything, dividing,
laughing out loud as I slept the sleep
of the winter frog, the parked bus.
When the third reversed into smudge
of protein, the first two grew
into planets. Do you remember
when I was a planet surrounding planets?
They pressed out; all matter in the multiverse
pressed in. I was a knot soaked overnight
in seawater. I stopped speaking completely then
for all the midnight barking, all the other utterances
lobbed skyward, but *in* me,
do you understand? As the snake
unhinges her jaw, so was I unhinged,
crowbarred. Fulcrum = this five-inch rent
above the bone-bridge. And then:
hyperspace tore through!
And it sounded like an unaccompanied
cello suite, like electric transformers
exploding in sequence up the ridge,
like what you hear inside the mud
when you rest a stethoscope there.
And today I hear everything
through that bedlam / that song.

KAIROS (CONCEPTION)

Rachel Moritz

The light from her hand, the window
shade flashing; delicate

faith that we are complete
by anyone's standards:

waiting for a pulse
from the gate—what isn't

stitching my body on the other side
of a blue drape

electric, visible,
yoked to someone

with a name.

How I've made
what we couldn't,

vials warming, gloved
trainer of chromosome,

spun in a bucket
from the well drawn up,

my own face inside.

CRAVING, FIRST MONTH

Heid E. Erdrich

My belly rejected everything but a certain sky,
the one that rocks the high north plains of my home.
Nothing but color and light for my mouth,
streaks of cirrus like pale lettuce—tear a leaf
and taste that clear covering of clouds!
I craved the prairie. Wild as Rapunzel's mother,
I would have paid the witch's price,
but my dear sister agreed to drive
into the horizon, north and north for hours,
the car skimming along the two-lane blacktop
between acres of flooded field. We were asea
in the land that bred us. It fed us and we were happy.
The rush of passing color like fuel—
waves of chartreuse—mustard weed lapping the ditches,
confusing waves of sky grown on earth—flax blue as mirage.
Then a doe, then her blazing fawn springing ahead of us
Red against the new crown of hard winter wheat.

That's what I grew my son on, month one.
I went hungry into the flat north
toward the reservation.
I ate it all.
Even the dusty green of the little-leaf sage
that covers my grandparents' grave
tasted good in my eyes.
Here it is, I said to the wind up the bald hill.
Here it is, I said to the question mark of child.
Here's the land we are born from. Here's what made us.
Here's the world that fed us. Here now, you eat too.

International Adoption Story: It Didn't Begin

Paige Riehl

with her crowning, the sweating
purple-blue burst through portal,
the head of black hair,
the arm reaching outward.

It didn't begin with despair
(or did it?). "Sign here":
three shaking pairs of hands
in two countries, icebergs between them.

Exacting is hard. The compass slips.
The pencil tip breaks. Perhaps it began
further back—the loving in dark beds
salt-saturated with hope.

No. Before that must have been
glimpses and glances,
hearts carried in pockets
and rubbed raw.

Our beginning is not. Not even
the winter day our baby's
unborn heart just stopped. Walk back
through the brambles of family,

climb through my own blood tree
and the sewn-on branch, the non-blood
(me), adopted (too) but that's not
when. (Not really.)

Whose beginning? Hers? Ours?
We are all wound tight,
loved and replayed replayed

then stuck, forced, and unfurled—

and I am standing here
at this dinner party with the taste
of dirt in my mouth. Everyone
waits for the answer.

Dear Daughter, Yes, We Are *Those* Kind of People

Amy Young

It was winter.
We were our own landscape
knees and shoulders naked as knobs,
breasts and buttocks atussle, backs
clean as granite blown by wind.
The Atlantic pushed and pulled around us.
Pebbles ground against each other
like gears or knuckles. Our tongues
probed crevices. The cliffs
bellowed with each seventh wave.
We wept and groaned and then we slept
into December, on through July.
Berries ripened. Blackberries, blueberries.
Constellations. An indigo sky.
The stars your fists and feet.
Yes, we did as bears and whales do.
The fruit was sweet.

HONEY

Arielle Greenberg

I am three months out and six to go,
stuffing my plastic Superball body with the salt
& twang of crackers die-cut into the shapes of fish.
God forsakes me when I forsake him
but mostly he's much kinder, as is his duty:
I am radiant, people tell me, and have no hives,
except the swarm of gold bombs biting its way
into my sticky hollow. And I don't mean sex.
I am just a menagerie for bright orange creatures.
Even my dreams are godless (and full
of God): I dream I am guided
by an elderly couple in a dim farmhouse
to their morning radio and blackberry tea
and then given the combs which I snap
into my dry mouth where they fill and fill.
Never, upon awaking, have I been so empty
and wanted more a cracker. Never so
suffused with the weekly, with time
as another god passing through the many perfect
crypts and ambers I house beneath my skin.

ULTRASOUND

Patricia Kirkpatrick

Sleeping raccoon face afloat in the stars,
someone has to show us how to see you.
Like children we look at the lit sky
to trace the spectacular and beloved constellation.
We say *heartbeat, head,* and *hand*
to mean the unglimpsed has departed
and journeys to Earth. To us. To begin
the effaced drift of creation again.
You were made on the Earth I remind myself.
Is your captivity bliss?
In the white repose
this picture gives
you could be on a porch swing,
some grainy dreamer looking out
to what the world might be
on this particular evening. Your sister lifts
her cup each night to cheer you.
Father clears the plates, Mother collapses
exhausted on the sofa.
It isn't perfect here.
The train goes by at ten,
its run a rumbled breathing for the sleepers.
I haven't walked the railroad tracks for years
nor picked lupine that grows between the ties.
But I know the smoky path
the divine mows across the sky
is the one you'll take.
Did you choose us? Or are you chosen
to light this fragile square of darkness?

for Anton

Peanut

Lorena Duarte

A tiny, end of your fingertip thing
to four-chambered and charted,
I have grown you a heart.
They map it out and it is correct:
blue, red.

I see fast-spinning bicycle wheels
in your future
and guitars
and girls or boys
that will test its proclivities.
Its poundings.

A spine and brain, 2 eyeballs too.

I have grown you a penis.
It is all very odd.

We have curled together,
nestled and soothed.

Already, I have gotten into the habit of rubbing your back.

We have:
grown hair together, grown fat together, well and lovely.

FUGUE: MATERNAL IMAGINATION

Heidi Czerwiec

> *"There are several things that cause monsters."*
> *– Ambroise Paré,* On Monsters & Marvels *(1585)*

Paré detailed legs fused fast as fish, spines
that bloom like split fruit, heads cleft or swelled
(Wyatt-to-be, awash inside his sea
of sound, sleeps on): "Profound grief or shock
that act upon the mother produce defect."
In ultrasound, the screen may or may not
a sequence of small tragedies unspool.
The tech measures, double-checks. *It is a Mercie*
(of God? Nature?) *when Births are not mis-formed.*

A sequence of small genetic tragedies
compounds, creates divine design, or error.
I've studied specimens. I know it's *Mercie*
when Births are not mis-formed, defects produced
(downloaded, they float across my screen) by grief.
Paré blamed a mother's fancy. Mine?
The birthmother's? What would her rape imprint
(Wyatt-to-be, awash inside his sea)?
God hath a speciall Hande in the wombe.

It was a shared mercy when Wyatt-to-be's mom
chose me, and when I chose to mother her son.
All adoptions are a sequence of small tragedies.
"Profound grief or shock that act upon
the mother produce defect." But which one?
Would it be fancy to beg the tech for lead
to shield him from the horrors in *my* head?
For months, I've studied fearful symmetries,
small tragedies who float—in wombs,
in jars, across a variety of screens.

Wyatt-to-be is pronounced perfect, divine
design or error. *It is a Mercie*
when Births are not mis-formed, I sigh to the screen.
Despite our tragedies, imagined and real,
Wyatt-to-be awash inside a sea of sound
exposes a perfect penis, then swims away
and waves, or seems to, as if to say

God hath a speciall Hande (what will He shape?).
And so hath Wyatt, waving at us all.

WITH CHILD

Joyce Sutphen

I used to live somewhere
far away from now,

and if you dug a hole straight
through the planet

you would have found me
on the other side

bare-legged in my blue denim
dress, my shape smooth and round

in the middle where the baby
curled upside down, sucking

her thumb. I used to sit
in the sun, rubbing a clay pot

with a silver spoon, carving
stems and leaves, watching

the clouds come over the hills,
and I used to feel the baby's

feet pushing on my ribs
and the skin stretching to fit her

turning, though I thought
that nothing would ever happen,

that there was no such country
where I would be delivered.

First Thought

Brenda Hillman

The first thought
was rage—

In certain systems, the point at which that thought
emerges from God's mind is his consort,
but before she turns her rage onto the world, the violent
lords must give her the body of a woman which is not easy.
Imagine them standing around before they will trap
God's vague thought into female flesh. The way
their robes undulate, the slightly yellowing raiment—

poor things.
They will not understand the rage.
It will be expressed forever in the split in things.
In the two-toned lupine,
in the cupped, silk lining of the tulip,
in the red and white of all armies in all wars,
it will bend over my dream wearing his face.

The moment my daughter was lifted
from me, that sticky
flesh screamed fury,
for she, too, blamed the female body—
I loved it that she screamed—

and I knew I had been sent to earth to understand that pain.

The nurses moved about, doing something
over to the left. Probably weighing her
on what looked like blue tin. The flash of non-
existence always at the edge of vision,
and in the next moment, some unasked-for radiance.

Under those lights,
the nurses seemed shabby—
the ivory lords, come haltingly
into the bridal chamber, slightly yellowing raiment.

The last pain on earth will not be the central pain,
it will be the pain of the soul and not the body,

the pain of the body will be long since gone,
absorbed into the earth, which made it beautiful—

don't you love the word raiment?
Dawn comes in white raiment.
Something like that.

No One Told Me I Would Fall in Love

Suzanne Swanson

He was backwards in me, blessed surprise, kept his secret til the midwife touched the wrong kind of cheek. I saw his little balls then, dwarfed in that huge mirror, almost fainted at the loss of a dream-daughter. I was naive, I let them take him across the room for all the numbers. They brought him back. I put him to my breast and it did not make their second-hands happy. They took him again, swaddled him, laid him in clear plastic, a stilted box at my bedside. And they called the doctor and he came in to have a look, and my baby whimpered and I reached over to jiggle the box and this guy I'd never met said *Yeah, you just keep doing that and he'll have you right where he wants you.* Hot love gushed in me then and I knew *if I want to jiggle my baby and he wants me to jiggle him, I'll jiggle my baby* and I looked at this man who didn't know me, didn't know my baby, and I jiggled the box and my sweet boy quieted and I lifted his bundled body into my arms before one more stranger might touch him.

NICU

Rachel Morgan

On the unit night nurses sing The Beatles
as they measure, hope, chart, and watch.
Mothers stroke their slackened bellies.
There is nothing to hold. Few things
are this sad. For the sickest, modern science
always needs to be moderner.

The Ancients thought the placenta
was the receptacle of the soul.
The Egyptians were so sure the soul
resided in the heart, brains were pulled
through the nose prior to mummification.
The post-modern soul is a series of chemical
reactions. Aristotle was correct: epigenesis
is the rise of order out of chaos. The process
usually goes right, each cell dividing perfectly
again and again. Except when it doesn't.

And my son. One day will I tell him this story,
that deep in his brain something misfired?

The first prayer was to let him breathe,
smile, and later walk. Now my greedy prayer
is that he learn to read novels, travel,
fall in love and stay that way, for wisdom,
to find work that brings goodness, to rejoice
in those first days each year of billowy fair-weather
clouds before fall, and die long after me.

Firstborn

Adrian Blevins

He was the wound who slithered through the wound I hadn't
    known was there.
He was a slur, he was wet: he was enormously inarticulate. Hairless
    and desolate

was he: in love with himself was he, he, he! Was he a ravenous,
    toothless snake

in a small pelt sheath? Was he a dragon, was he a fawn? His
    cloistered bones
were made of stars and his tiny eyes were tiny stars: my
    cunt-his-starship

was now, however, a lion: we couldn't say which of us was roaring
    more.

O Mother, I saw robins there, as it was March. O Mother it was
    March
when he devoured me. Or maybe that's erroneous and what
    happened was

he got a will. Maybe what happened was he opened his eyes for the
    milk to swill

to swell those bones until he was the tower and he was the lion. I'd
    watch at midnight
for incisors. He'd call at midnight to say there was Budweiser there

and girls in short-shorts: there were grottos there, and into the
    grottos

he would slink. O Mother, what animal or spirit is he? O Mother,
from whence could it come—from whence did he come—but me?

What I Think About When Someone Uses "Pussy" as a Synonym for "Weak"

Beth Ann Fennelly

At the deepest part of the deepest part, I rocked shut like a stone. I'd climbed as far inside me as I could. Everything else had fallen away. Midwife, husband, bedroom, world: quaint concepts. My eyes were clamshells. My ears were clapped shut by the palms of the dead. My throat was stoppered with bees. I was the fox caught in the trap, and I was the trap. Chewing off a leg would have been easier than what I now required of myself. I understood I was alone in it. I understood I would come back from there with the baby, or I wouldn't come back at all. I was beyond the ministrations of loved ones. I was beyond the grasp of men. Even their prayers couldn't penetrate me. The pain was such that I made peace with that. I did not fear death. Fear was an emotion, and pain had scalded away all emotions. I chose. In order to come back with the baby, I had to tear it out at the root. Understand, I did this without the aid of my hands.

BREASTS

Heid E. Erdrich

One day I looked down
Imagine my shame
Bustin' out!
The blank buds
Have produced
Both nipples
Years later
The left more blind
My winking chest
Though boys groped,
Called me Chesty.
I never could grasp.
Some availability?

Their true power,
I learned as I nursed.
Or even among friends,
Only you and the babe

And there they were
Just twelve or eleven
Where were they before?
I wore so long could not
Such abundance.
Inverted, I heard
From my male midwife
Than the bright-eyed right.
I hardly dared blush
Made horrible jokes
Why they fixed on me
Did my size advertise
I avoided sweaters for years.

Not to attract but to repel,
Whip them out in public
You will clear the room.
And the peace breasts make.

We Just Want It To Be Healthy

Cullen Bailey Burns

Here is the little bomb. We call it baby,
all mouth and potential. We do not speak
of disappointments—no one to strap it on yet
and cross the border, the demilitarized zone
of our foyer. The neighbors coo at it, rub
the tops of its dimpled hands with their thumbs
and say, "give me a smile."
We think about schools and such, of course.
But at night when we lay our plans
it always kicks its feet from the bassinet
in the corner of the room, central to everything,
central to some final detonation.

BREAKING SILENCE—FOR MY SON

Patricia Fargnoli

The night you were conceived
your father drove up Avon Mountain
and into the roadside rest stop
that looked over the little city,
its handful of scattered sparks.
I was eighteen and thin then
but the front seat of the 1956 Dodge
seemed cramped and dark,
the new diamond I hadn't known
how to refuse trapping flecks of light.
Even then the blackness was thick
as a muck you could swim through.
Your father pushed me down
on the scratchy seat, not roughly
but as if staking a claim,
and his face rose like
a thin-shadowed moon above me.
My legs ached in those peculiar angles,
my head bumped against the door.
I know you want me to say I loved him
but I wanted only to belong—to anyone.
So I let it happen,
the way I let all of it happen—
the marriage, his drinking, the rage.
This is not to say I loved you any less—
only I was young and didn't know yet
we can choose our lives.
It was dark in the car.
Such weight and pressure,
the wet earthy smell of night,
a slickness like glue.
And in a distant inviolate place,
as though it had nothing at all
to do with him, you were a spark
in silence catching.

At Last, She Is Finished with Emptiness

Katie Bickham

After slow months of healing, night
nursing, the breast pump, burying
the old, faithful dog, board meetings, cursing
the monitor, the hurrying, three-minute showers
and half-hour naps and instant breakfasts,
finally, her husband who can wait

no longer leads her up the worn stairs
to the sanctuary of rumpled bedding. He guides her
mouth onto him, tilts her backwards,
reopens her softly, a storm door creaking
in sunlight after long darkness. She hears the crack
of a bat; a crowd cheers at the ballpark

down the street. She imagines the sweating
fans cheer for her, that the jays and robins
herald her coming, that she is being urged,
egged on by the whole waking universe. Yes. At last,
she is saying yes again, summering, ready again
to belong to the boy and to the man.

Afterwards, she tells him a year's worth
of secrets. Then they hear the blankets rustle,
a babble over the monitor. Sirens sing
their songs from both sides, to hold them
there, to make them rise, promise such silence
and noise and thirst and wetness, more than enough.

Mother Load

LEAVING HOME AT TWO

Sigi Leonhard

when we go places now
she sits next to me in her car seat
her brow wrinkled as if
in deep, unsettling thought
and, through her pacifier, says:
on the road again

we have survived the trip
of early babyhood
we haven't slept in two years
kept up by croup and crankiness
but come out on the other side
basically intact

she notices everything
alike in our quirks, we love
each other's company
after a quick glance
at me, she says, pacifier
hanging from the side of her mouth
like a cigar:
you forgot your lipstick

as we pull out of the driveway
the car revs up exuberantly
she says: when I was little
I sat in a different car seat

Raw

Michelle Matthees

And so in we went to Miracle Mart,
her first American supermarket.
Yes, that was its real name. No

effort was made at translation. She
shopped with care, lifting and turning
each piece of produce; note:

how things look is important. She
searched for slits in a too-tight
skin, the sad nothing of a bruise.

"Ya xachu," *I want*, she said lifting
the solid green shot-put of a squash
high into the air, where it wavered.

Twice she rapped on it definitively
with her knuckles. I was glad
to see her being so careful,

so smart about food, beaming,
her face a moon
just able to rise above the cart.

She pushed the cart in black boots
with undone tongues that flapped.
Powdered milk was next, *I want*. Ick,

I thought, but okay. The red
Carnation fell into the cart.
We left the meat alone,

checked out, drove home. Joy
in unpacking! She played. I sliced
the squash, disturbed slumbering

seeds. I set the oven. "Shto Dyelayesh?" *What
are you doing?* she asked and took
a wedge of raw squash and bit into it.

"Tam," *like this.* I kept the cold
I felt inside. Same for the milk:
straight from the box with a spoon,

no water or heat, just a face full
of construction-like dust. A plain
bird alit in the ornamental

shrub. We stood in the vast
prairie kitchen where it
would be a while until dinner.

KNOTS

Linda Pastan

In the receding tide
of light,
among bulrushes
and eelgrass
my small son teaches
my stuttering hands
the language of sailor's knots.

I tell him how
each Jewish bride
was given a knotted chaos
of yarn
and told to order it
into a perfect sphere,
to prove she'd be a patient wife.

Patient, impatient son
I've unknotted shoestrings,
kitestrings, tangled hair.
But standing at high windows
enclosed in the domestic rustle
of birds and leaves
I've dreamed of knotting
bedsheets together
to flee by.

Things You Didn't Put on Your Resumé

Joyce Sutphen

How often you got up in the middle of the night
when one of your children had a bad dream,

and sometimes you woke because you thought
you heard a cry but they were all sleeping,

so you stood in the moonlight just listening
to their breathing, and you didn't mention

that you were an expert at putting toothpaste
on tiny toothbrushes and bending down to wiggle

the toothbrush ten times on each tooth while
you sang the words to songs from *Annie*, and

who would suspect that you know the fingerings
to the songs in the first four books of the Suzuki

Violin Method and that you can do the voices
of Pooh and Piglet especially well, though

your absolute favorite thing to read out loud is
Bedtime for Frances and that you picked

up your way of reading it from Glynnis Johns,
and it is, now that you think of it, rather impressive

that you read all of Narnia and all of the Ring Trilogy
(and others too many to mention here) to them

before they went to bed and on the way out to
Yellowstone, which is another thing you don't put

on the resumé: how you took them to the ocean
and the mountains and brought them safely home.

Long Nights

Connie Wanek

> *It's good to have poems that begin with tea*
> *and end with God.*
> *— Robert Bly*

A cup forgotten on the windowsill,
half full of cold tea, half of moonlight.
The rocking chair sits alone now,
its back erect and its seat ample.
There I nursed the first baby, and read
the *Alexandria Quartet*, wherein
a child was a further romance.
I still feel her in my arms, limp with sleep,
and see her heartbeat in her fontanel.
Whenever I tried to lay her in her crib
her eyes flew open. Let her cry, they said.
But I never let her cry.

My mother carried six of us,
one after the other, on her hip,
as we descended from her embrace
to our stations on the earth. She says
to this day her left hip is higher,
her left arm brutally strong,
her right infinitely dexterous.
Long were the nights she spent in labor
wrestling babies from the Creator.

So Like Her Father

Connie Wanek

> *A glorious young bamboo has sprung up overnight!*
> *– Issa*

My daughter sits cross-legged
on the tabletop and reads to me
as I wash the floor on my hands and knees.
Through an open door we smell the first lilacs.

In autumn she will leave this house.
I will never say the words
I remember from my father:
"When you return it will be as a visitor."

Still there exists a natural order
less compromising than our love, or hers,
or the love I bear my parents.

I scrub with water mixed with tears
and the footprints come away.
"I'm sorry," I say, "I wasn't listening."
She takes a sip of tea and begins again.

The Curse of Color

Sherry Quan Lee

> *We are never free from the feeling that we have failed. We are never free from self-loathing. We are never free from the feeling that something is wrong with us, not with the world that made this mess.*
> — *Jesmyn Ward,* Men We Reaped

If I could have imagined my brown babies suffering
would I have said no?

Would I have pushed back, kept my legs crossed,
the cross of motherhood not salvation?

   * * *

I couldn't bring my babies forward
as I dreamt them—beyond poverty, beyond race.

I'm not going to apologize.

I can't stop them from trudging in muck stuck
in my fate, my phantom scars spread
like sadness, like grief.

Everyone (white) seems
so happy, so accomplished,
so very, very good.

   * * *

I am seeing with a mad eye, perplexed.
Mothers can give what they can give:
I tried to give more.

Is it anger I feel when
I compare their wealth to mine?

   * * *

Have I cursed my sons
with the truth? I am not white.

Mother warned me.

Heat Stroked

Heidi Czerwiec

> *I drowned in the fire of having you,*
> *I burned in the river of not having you.*
> — *Robert Pinsky, "Antique"*

Exhausted, I smell exhaust. Electrical scent of ozone. Burnt meat. Bonfire-char. Small spasms in my migrained brain hallucinate a veritable catalogue of flamed smells and smoke. I have to ask Do you smell that? I have to hunt a source outside my mind because what if? I never pass out from the pain of it so I'm usually awake when the smells come. When the smells come in the middle of the night, when the family sleeps, I have to hunt ever harder because what if?

The middle of the night is a former flame; with an infant I see too much of it. Wee hours, wee one, low lamps and the allure of lit screens all make my migraines flare. When not to cries, I awake to ghosts of wood smoke and scorched plaster and shorted fuses. Either way I lumber the halls because what if? what if?

And what if it all burned? What if my son burnt up, burnt away? Would my unmothering life lie beneath, awaiting me to brush off ash?

He cries in his crib, teething and febrile. I cry in my bed, migraining and feeble, pain that will not let me pass out, pain that smells pleasantly of mesquite. We cry, immolating and unconsumed.

Child, you suck the air from me, yet I burn more brightly for it.

Yours

Sonia Greenfield

Suppose he was yours who saw rust
at first turn of the green wheel handle,
   your yard slicked down, sprinklers
ticking away days meted out in trips
   to 7-Eleven & the community pool.
Suppose he was yours who saw brown,
   waited for it to run clear, then drank
down the whole metallic feel of it
   from the copper end of a hose, summer
spread before him like a growing puddle.
   Suppose he was yours who bathed
in the river in your tub, scratched until
   his skin oxidized, flaking off in his sheets.
Suppose you saw pinpricks of his blood
   but washed those sheets in the same water
anyway. Suppose they said boil it,
   & you did, but that only made it worse.
Suppose he was yours who was told
   his anger will fleck & spread unchecked,
was told bits of heavy metal will damn
   his lobes. Suppose he was yours who
was tested & told he will lose himself
   in a wash so sick everyone already knew
you couldn't eat the fish caught there.
   Suppose he said *I'm just going to be stupid
anyway.* What would well up in you,
   & where would that poison run to?

Hurry

Marie Howe

We stop at the dry cleaners and the grocery store
and the gas station and the green market and
Hurry up honey, I say, hurry,
as she runs along two or three steps behind me
her blue jacket unzipped and her socks rolled down.

Where do I want her to hurry to? To her grave?
To mine? Where one day she might stand all grown?
Today, when all the errands are finally done, I say to her,
Honey I'm sorry I keep saying Hurry—
you walk ahead of me. You be the mother.

And, Hurry up, she says, over her shoulder, looking
back at me, laughing. Hurry up now darling, she says,
hurry, hurry, taking the house keys from my hands.

Marks

Linda Pastan

My husband gives me an A
for last night's supper,
an incomplete for my ironing,
a B plus in bed.
My son says I am average,
an average mother, but if
I put my mind to it
I could improve.
My daughter believes
in Pass/Fail and tells me
I pass. Wait 'til they learn
I'm dropping out.

PARTUS SEQUITUR VENTREM

Teri Ellen Cross Davis

> *A Latin phrase that stands for the principle that the*
> *children of an enslaved woman are themselves born as*
> *slaves and owned by their mother's master.*

I. Morning

His knobby six-year-old knees,
his anxious pace as if to keep step
with the questions' steady overflow:
"Is there a giant octopus in the Bermuda Triangle?"
"How is paper made?"
"How do fireworks know when to explode?"
No one told me black boys could burn
so bright. Wait, I am wrong, the dark sky
has seen their fire snuffed by white hoods,
malevolent blue eyes in bluer uniforms,
white women's screams—all have been match
to their tinder wood. So I hug my son tight.
Kiss the curl cropped so close it's straight.
My mother-eye insatiable, he is dessert
and I'll always have seconds. Each morning
I lick my thumb, clean him up good, wishing
in vain the amniotic sac had dried to armor.

II. Night

His lisp, loose, syrupy-sweet,
sneaks into my ear. Feel its heat,
small source more flicker than
flame, flanked by arms still
dreaming of muscle. He claims
my squishy stomach *the best pillow.*
If the security of our locked arms
could extend beyond growth spurts,
clocks, calendars, to the someone

interviewing him, to the someone
following him in the store, to the
someone holding my son's life
in trembling fingers poised above
a phone's keypads—let my love
be a note safety-pinned to his chest
—*send him back alive, unharmed.*
As a black mother in America,
I know my wails are birthright,
pinned with iron,
penned in ink.

Waiting Up

Maryann Corbett

Not home. Not home yet. Four A.M. Unknot me,
God whom I less than half believe my help.
Damp down the pounding underneath my scalp.
Unhook the gut-tight line of fear that's caught me
listening for cars, oh me of little faith.
They've seized their own lives, laughing, "Go to bed!"
And God, I hate her—hate the hag in my head
who mutters, praying through her gritted teeth,
make them come home, come home. God, shut her up.
Let me believe the thousand times they've come
home safe will make the door click one more time
and lock behind them. Free me from the trap
of thinking your ideas of *safe* and *home*
might not (my God!) be anything like mine.

Oblation

Leslie Adrienne Miller

In the dank hole of the locker room,
I unbuckle the straps from under his skates,
lift the hard globe from his head,
and slip the dripping wedge from his teeth.

Trying hard to be supportive of this sport,
I snap a picture of his moist curls fresh
from the cave of the helmet, cheeks
stippled with risen blood, eyes flashing

with blue exertion. But a man across
the locker room stops me. No pictures
allowed. By which I suddenly understand
that someone could be here for illicit thrill,

boys ripe with sweat, packing sodden gear
in bags they cannot lift without adults.
I think of my boy's bliss at owning
his first nut cup, and how it isn't me

he wants to help him unlace the skates
but his father, or failing that, any
of the dozen burly strangers milling
in the hall. I've given my only son

to this company of men who crave
the white and unforgiving oval of the rink,
who grunt and dive for the chance to add
their mayhem to the fray. They all adore

the rush to punch a cuneiform of dents
against the boards, the spray of shards
that blasts from the blade's bright veer
and flies in the caged face of the foe.

CROSSING GUARD

Sheila Packa

At eleven,
my son was a crossing guard
with orange mesh vest
striped with glowing neon tape.
He dropped a flag
to stop the stream of cars for the children
on the corner.
Then he was innocent, with blond hair
and a tiny gold earring on the ear,
not pierced but looking as if it were.

If I'd been a school girl coming to his corner
with my heavy book bag,
I'd have thought the earring
something to be proud of
just as much as the uniform.

If I'd been the boy in the desk ahead of his
who turned around
and saw the earring on his nostril
and turned back quickly to see
if the teacher saw
I would have never told.

But I was the mother and so came
to the corner the way that mothers do,
reaching for his shoulder, trying
to hold him back from the world.

As he signaled and brought the traffic
to a halt, I crossed
without even knowing it
from youth into middle age
and he went from childhood into that world
that men must live in.

BOUNCE

Lorena Duarte

It was the only way to keep you happy, that and the hair dryer but the hairdryer has burnt out so it's back to bouncing, non-stop, don't stop. Bounce, bounce, bounce. My back gives out and on I keep: bounce, bounce, bounce. Strapped to my chest, and put back in your fetal trance. Bounce, bounce, bounce.

I don't blame you. The world is made of hissing wind and honking horns. Barks. Plastic crinkling. They all put you on edge, on and over. And so I bounce.

Today, almost 3 years later, I am bouncing you on a toy pony. One of those old-fashioned deals. Today, you looked up at your speech therapist, then me, and said "mo," your word for "more." And so I bounced you "mo."

How many lessons to get you to this point? How, after those first few months of non-stop screaming, you became silent. A still stone. No bounce. You were quiet for a year. No bounce.

Today, you're relearning your first love. Today you snort-laugh and I cheer your every sound.

You still cry when the bouncing stops.

There I am, you strapped to my chest, wearing the yoga ball out. There I am, bouncing you on an old chipped horse.

Bounce,
        bounce,
                bounce.

WHEN SHE TAKES MY BODY INTO HER BODY
from "Latching On, Falling Off"

Beth Ann Fennelly

She comes to me squirming in her father's arms,
gumming her fingers, her blanket, or rooting
on his neck, thrashing her mouth from side to side
to raise a nipple among his beard hairs. My shirt sprouts
two dark eyes; for three weeks she's been outside me,
and I cry milk to hear my baby—any baby—cry.

In the night, she smells me. From her bassinet
she wakes with a squall, her mouth impossibly huge,
her tongue aquiver with anger the baby book says
she doesn't have, aquiver like the clapper of a bell.
Her passion I wasn't prepared for, her need
naked as a sturgeon with a rippling, red gill.

Who named this *letdown*, this tingling upswing?
A valve twists, the thin opalescence spurts past the gate,
then comes the hindcream to make my baby creamyfat.
I fumble with one hand at my bra, offer the target
of my darkened nipple, with the other hand steady
her too-heavy head. She clamps on, the wailing ceases.

No one ever mentioned she's out for blood. I wince
as she tugs milk from ducts all the way to my armpits.
It hurts like when an angry sister plaits your
hair. It hurts like that, and like that you desire it.
Soon, soon—I am listening—she swallows,
and a layer of pain kicks free like a blanket.

Tethered, my womb spasms, then, lower, something shivers.
Pleasure piggybacks the pain, though it, too,
isn't mentioned, not to the child, now drunk and splayed
like a hobo, not to the sleeping husband, innocent beside us.
Let me get it right so I remember: Once, I bared my chest
and found an animal. Once, I was delicious.

MOTHERS

Deborah Keenan

The one who begs forgiveness, the one eating the smallest
piece of meat at dinner, uneasy carnivore.

The one lifting the baby to see the moon, the one who helps
the baby see the moon any night without clouds.

She buys the same things at the grocery store each week,
chooses the wrong cereal, redeems herself, reads out loud

past bedtime to the child with tired eyes, the child who
wept, "I said Frosted Flakes, not Corn Pops. Never Corn Pops."

The mother who sees the future, each child adrift, and herself
powerless, the mother playing rock-and-roll songs while children

wait for their turn at the stereo. The mother with too much
to do can't stop listening to STOP MAKING SENSE, the mother

who knows all the words by heart, the mother who doesn't own
her heart too often, the one washing out her son's shirt

by hand after the acrylic paint exploded backwards out of the
tube he held bent over his painting, the mother who rages,

who throws the Kirby vacuum cleaner down the stairs, screams
into the beloved child's face, "I can't do it for you, you must

care about yourself," the one who's read *Jane Eyre* too many times,
the one looking for privacy, the one who smokes the cigarette,

and the one who's always quitting smoking, the one who's never
lost a child, the one who holds the dying child, and gives her

mind away to the sky, the dirt. The mother cannot let the child die and be called mother, so when the child dies the mother

gives her mind away and does not understand what she is holding in her hands.

The Perfect Mother

Susan Griffin

1

The perfect mother lets the cat
sleep on her head. The
children laugh.
Where is she?
She is not carefully ironing the starched
ruffles of a Sunday dress.
What does she say?
She does not speak.
Her head is under the cat and
like the cat, she sleeps.

2

But her children are in a marsh!
Bogged, they have gone wild.
Yet, no one should worry.
See, they are there, in a sunny kitchen.
They drink cups of soup and wipe
their faces with yellow napkins.
What does it matter if
they are hatching plots, if
in their waking dreams
the poor cat is trapped
its hair
standing on end?

3

Where shall we go? We ask the perfect
mother. What
do you want of us? She is no

where to be found.
Not in the cookie jar
we have broken to bits
not under the shiny kitchen floor
not on our lips.
Here we are transfixed,
mourning the perfect mother, and she
is caught in the trapped cat
of her children's dreams.

THE BAD MOTHER

Susan Griffin

The bad mother wakes from dreams
of imperfection trying to be perfection.
All night she's engineered a train
too heavy with supplies
to the interior. She fails.
The child she loves
has taken on bad habits, cigarettes
maybe even drugs. She
recognizes lies. *You don't
fool me*, she wants to say,
the bad mother, ready to play
and win.
This lamb who's gone—
this infant she is
pinioned—does not listen,
she drives with all her magic down a
different route to darkness where
all life begins.

Love, the Final Healer

Roberta Hill

for Jacob

We unstuck a walking stick walking
down a wall and shoved it into a jar
where it hung, a crooked finger.
You slept through the night
while I had the nightmare:
It snuck out through an airhole
and grew to a kitten's size.
I felt its suction feet smacking
up my arm and woke to see
a tree limb with shrewd eyes
arch its back over half my life.
Son, we've little time and much to learn.

The April you were nine months old
a meadowlark in the cottonwood near Mission
forgot her name
and courageously sang at three a.m.
Birdsong in darkness rippling my world
beyond reservation borders and the Nebraska line,
I went out to find her
above the scraps of snow
and came back, fully alive,
to dishes greying in the sink. I wanted
to be happy, but the screen tore and curled,
the nails cried in the walls,
the heater failed, and winter blustered back,
stronger than ever.

Scared and hot, you fussed for hours
in the light of a motel,
too dark to be a home, too full of unknown noise.
We're caught in some old story.
I'm the woman winter loved

and you, the son of winter, ask
where did he go and why.
This poem gets cut to just one sentence:
You grow old enough and I get wise.
Yes, the days ride stallions
and leave us in the dust,
yet the details of these days
must imply a different ending.

When we drove through Minnesota, your toes
ate summer air. On an Oklahoma hill,
we poked a puffball with a stick.
Its spore vanished into blackjacks,
a forest just your size.
In Riverton, Wyoming, I wouldn't buy that rock,
bland as the staring rancher in the Teton Coffee Shop.
We could fly to Equator. Customs there differ.
Families are so big and poor that fathers pray
for just one wife. Instead let's accept
the hallways we've walked
toward a winter ripe with ozone,
toward changing drifts of flowers.

What can I teach you that the sun
doesn't show, caring for the sky?
He puts on cloud pajamas, returns with bird
and early blue. What rhythms do I know
that would match water? When it chants,
the frogs and fish experience the world as one.
The wind reveals far more tricks
as you cartwheel in the semi-dark
under a half-moon and your favorite star.
I can only whisper what I'm learning still,
what the trees completely understand.

After every turn of innocence and loss,
in the awful stillnesses to come,

when we give what's true and deep,
from the original in ourselves,
love, the final healer, makes certain
that we grow. A bug, a bird, a phrase
from some old story or a friend will find us.
Then we'll remember winter as a cleansing
like a note held high and long
above a vast terrain. As we walk,
we'll see the yellow butterflies
lighting on the alfalfa, working on the wind.

Tides Rush Through

What Is Supposed to Happen

Naomi Shihab Nye

When you were small,
we watched you sleeping,
waves of breath
filling your chest.
Sometimes we hid behind
the wall of baby, soft cradle
of baby needs.
I loved carrying you between
my own body and the world.

Now you are sharpening pencils,
entering the forest of
lunch boxes, little desks.
People I never saw before
call out your name
and you wave.

This loss I feel,
this shrinking,
as your field of roses
grows and grows . . .

Now I understand history.
Now I understand my mother's
ancient eyes.

Into Autumn

Saymoukda Duangphouxay Vongsay

I remember the hallway smelled
of pan-fried sunny-side-up eggs
the night that I flushed your older
could've-been brother, could've-been sister
down the toilet.

I had to explain to your now-grandmother
and now-grandfather
it was the size of an avocado seed.
I say this while I extend my palm up,
making an empty cup.

It would've been born into autumn,
a time when trees understand the letting go of leaves.

And you.
I don't remember how the room smelled
the afternoon you were born into autumn.

The only thing that mattered
was no fear of having to let go.

ELEGY FOR THE THING I LOST WITH HER

Jennifer Manthey

She was four and he just a
months-old baby. He never slept.
From two to six a.m., I walked with
him through the museum of our
home. He looked at the smoky
starlight through sheer curtains and
smiled. The slope of the attic ceiling
and smiled. The pattern of cats and
little homes on the chair we were
given for free and smiled. His eyes
were ancient and reptile. His mouth
was always open; his alien fingers
working. If I laid down, he cried. If I
walked, he smiled. It was like being
calmly tortured with a flower. And at
seven a.m., when he and I finally
drifted, she came lightly running to my
bedside with her bright *Good
morning*!
      My whispers were wild
and desperate. Don't wake your
brother! All my sweetness was drained
from me—I did this many times. Go
downstairs! Go see Daddy! Her face
dulling. I wanted half an hour more,
fifteen minutes even. Soon, she stayed
each morning in her room until I came
to get her.

SLOW FOOD

Autumn Stephens

By the time I unpack
the hospital bag
the baby is eating meat.

His Speed and Strength

Alicia Suskin Ostriker

His speed and strength, which is the strength of ten
years, races me home from the pool.
First I am ahead, Niké, on my bicycle,
no hands, and the *Times* crossword tucked in my rack,
then he is ahead, the Green Hornet,
buzzing up Witherspoon,
flashing around the corner to Nassau Street.

At noon sharp he demonstrated his neat
one-and-a-half flips off the board:
Oh, brave. Did you see me, he wanted to know.
And I doing my backstroke laps was Juno
Oceanus, then for a while I watched some black
and white boys wrestling and joking, teammates, wet
plums and peaches touching each other as if

it is not necessary to make hate,
as if Whitman was right and there is no death.
A big wind at our backs, it is lovely, the maple boughs
ride up and down like ships. Do you mind
if I take off, he says. I'll catch you later,
see you, I shout and wave, as he peels
away, pedaling hard, rocket and pilot.

SOMETHING YOU WILL NEED

Diane Jarvenpa

for my daughter

A map.
Yours. Use it.
Only you can know
how the roads will turn,
switch back, climb.
Only you can read its latitudes,
trace your finger along the relief route,
steer your way on blue highways.
Go ahead, study those junctions,
rotate directionally
sun/moon mountain/sea,
plot your course
along mineral brooks,
witch hazel woods.
Devise your own whistle stops,
track your own epi-center,
thumbtack only the towns that matter.
Take your monk's pen
and draw an illumination of cypress or peacocks.
You might keep aware of scale and curvature,
but only if continental drift is involved.
Just remember your projection
will not need to be conventional.
Line up the quadrants
to meet up with the sweet and spice folds,
to find the finest donuts, hottest salsa.
Use as rain shield, Ouija board,
paperback of fables, periodic vector
of wanderings and intentions,
humble candle of transit,
talisman of bearings.
Destination,
a voluminous theory

that keeps expanding,
an artful goal.
If you need to circle back,
fortify, mend.
I will draw this dot
here by the center rib,
the world before the journey,
carried safe in the soft, dark cloth
of your pocket.

Driving My Son Twelve Hundred Miles to College

Julia Klatt Singer

The fog that lifts from the morning hills of Wisconsin, the sunlight
that breaks its way into the roof of one of the many dozen
falling down barns. The flock of birds that fly a dance just for us,
two white moths mirroring each other's thoughts, the caramel
fawn propped in the ditch. My: *don't run*. Billboards for faded
industries, dusty forgotten desires. Chicago, in the rearview
mirror. Truck stops selling stick ponies, rhinestone-studded
baseball caps, lighters and gasoline. Field after field after field of
corn, of soybeans, more corn. The hum of tires on asphalt. The
semi-truck and trailer lying on its side in the ditch. The black bear
curled as if in sleep on the dotted-white line, my small prayer for it.
The names: Black River Falls, South Bend, Elyria, Gary, Sandusky,
Toledo. The blue-green of morning. The silver lingering of dusk.
The hours. What we said to each other. All of it. A blur.

EMPTY NEXT SYNDROME

Paula Cisewski

Then came the day
I had to relearn how
to inhabit both my name and
my home, for my son had moved out. How
well he'd grown.

I can force *it*-ness on
myself. When *it* is me.
When I am a person.
A personal
Person-object.

Dwelling in general became more
relic-like. I ghosted around
in different rooms, my body simply
housing a former avocation's vacancy.

Incarnate,
it/I could disappear,
Separated here and united
there in multifarious
congress.

I still had a name and when I went out, I
was called by it, but it sounded wrong for a
long time, unnecessary: a battery
corroding in an engine

When *it* considers itself
a fully judge-able object,
it creates narratives
immoderately, like
charming verdicts: story after

or an unexamined belief. How is it useful
simply to cart
a single personal name around
from private to public spaces?

story, like a cut bud
in a vase, the traditional
arc subsumed by a fetish
for dwelling solely
on the denouement.

How is it maternal,
or even part of
my value system?

It began with me.
It is now
nothing.

MUD, GRASS, AND TWIGS AS IN A TREE: DAY ONE: FRAGMENTS

Jeanne Lutz

It's only eight forty-three
and I think I might die from this.

Before he went off to college yesterday
my son left me a note on the fridge:
thanks for taking care of my iguana—love you!
his handwriting like a one-armed butcher's,
but I know his love for me is true as raw meat.

I flutter around my vacant nest
mending and defending,
this is, after all, what awareness means,
learning to be more kindlier company,
as if I were somebody I was fond of
and hoped to encourage.

The cat, old and phobic,
a Greta Garbo in her final days,
stays behind the jacquard couch.

I visit an uncle in the nursing home
where people in wheelchairs
are parked in the halls, abandoned
like cars on the side of the road.

I am an Edvard Munch painting,
not screaming on a bridge or anything,
just green and distorted, cooking
in a kitchen with too many plates.

My husband comes home
from work and tells me

that this chicken pot pie
is the best chicken pot pie
he has ever tasted. He tells me
I am beautiful, takes my hand,
and reminds me that our son
will be home for Thanksgiving.

Thanksgiving is a thousand light years away.

The last thing I want to be to anyone
is a complete fix-it-upper, but I can't
help it and start crying for all the people
I have already lost
and for all the people I know
I will lose in the future.

I call my mother. I mean it, I say.
I think I am going to die from this.

You won't, she promises, her wisdom
a hymn, her heart an aria,
and her voice a fine folk tune
telling me everything will be okay,
even when you don't know
what okay even looks like.

BELOVED MATH

Paula Cisewski

Someone who has gone remains for all time
　　　(*How does one keep? One keeps*
the Sabbath.) Someone who equals speechlessness, isn't right outside
while a boy's cabinet of speechlessness longs.
Below the earth's surface like a refused god:
this someone is equal to or greater than the absence of light.

As mother and son discover the lightness
of the ways we don't need someone, time
wears us like two strung beads around the neck of a god.
　　　(*How does one keep? One keeps*
the books.) Speechlessness is long.
We are in our home and someone isn't outside

waiting for us to open up. For us to go outside
where things remain which a boy can't study under lamplight.
I must praise his innate talent for long
negative numbers. The beloved math of his lifetime,
without someone, a remainder. (*One keeps*
a precious thing, a keep-sake.) An ungodly

sum of things to possibly lose! Good lord
am I the crazy mother who cooks for an army? Outside
there is an army. (*Someone in particular repeatedly keeps*
not coming back.) Tired of discovering the lightness
of the ways we don't need someone, how it multiplies, time
still happens to us. The boy's grown lanky

within the duration of an absence, his private belonging.
Tall as someone, he waits for his first kiss like an impatient god
of love. A classic, grass-stained figure. (*Sometimes*
I suspect k-e-e-p has stopped being a word.) He goes outside

to join every other boy who happens in the daylight.
(*How does one keep? A mother keeps*

house / refuses to keep
house.) Long
after the subtraction of daylight
hours still pass through us, goading
us on. We don't stop going outside
because someone unexpected isn't there every time.

(*Keepkeepkeep. It doesn't even sound right.*) Christ
a long time goes by like a parade outside.
I am forever lighting, then extinguishing, our lamps.

COLD

Ellen Bass

On this early morning in Vancouver, my son and I stop
on our way to breakfast when we hear
the Kenyan will soon be running past this corner.
Of course we want to see his gorgeous stride,
but after half an hour I'm shivering
in my thin sweater. That's when my son begins
to rub my back—offering up the heat of his palms.
What could be better than to stand here hungry
and be curried like this? If I hadn't been cold
I wouldn't have his hands on my spine,
flaring across my shoulder blades. For a moment
it seems possible that every frailty, every pain,
could be an opening, a crack that lets the unexpected
reach us. How can I remember this
when I'm old and need so much?

On Climbing Petroglyphs

Kimberly Blaeser

I.

Newly twelve with size seven feet
dangling beside mine off the rock ledge,
legerdemain of self knowledge.
How do I say anything—magic
words you might need to hear?
With flute-playing, green-painted nails
your child's fingers reach to span the range
of carmel-colored women in our past.
Innocently you hold those ghost hands:
each story a truce we've made with loss.
How can I tell you there were others?

Big-boned women who might try
to push out hips in your runner's body.
Women who will betray you for men,
a bottle, or because they love you
love you, don't want to see you disappointed
in life, so will hold you, hold you hostage
with words, words tangled around courage
duty or money. When should I show you
my own flesh cut and scarred on the barbs
of belonging and love's oldest language?

II.

No, let us dangle here yet, dawdle
for an amber moment while notes shimmer
sweetly captured in turquoise flute songs—
the score of a past we mark together.
No words whispered yet beyond these painted

untainted rock images of ancients: sun, bird, hunter.
Spirit lines that copper us to an infinity.
Endurance. Your dangling. Mine.
Before the floor of our becoming.
Perhaps even poets must learn silence,
that innocence, that space before speaking.

Linked Like Sand to Tides

What No One Tells You

Tracy Youngblom

Their lips form the soft Os of hunger
even in sleep. They pout involuntarily,

so skip the self-doubt. Some
cries are just for attention, not alarm.

Some will drool, souring fabric
and hugs for years. Breast milk looks

thin, but it's thick enough to dry
in stiff circles on all your shirts.

They will refuse the breast, eventually.
You may be ready. Maybe not.

They will interrupt you
in the bathroom and in profound

sleep. They will run and scream
down grocery aisles to make sure

you are paying attention. They will
eat wildly, scattering rice grains

on the floor like sticky petals.
They will lie to you, grinning.

They will not be satisfied until
they have eaten through your pantry

and your heart and even then
you will still want more.

Family Bed

Teri Ellen Cross Davis

Her first tumult, roundhouse, flip
little spark of flutter, little slip
when the universe tumbled through me
I plodded, heavy with importance, our
path forward. Now she curls to me
the little c to the S curve of my breast,
my nipple a breath away from her
needy lips. You say we must break her
of sleeping with mommy—with daddy.
You say two nights of no rest, of offering myself
is two nights too many—but she beckons
and when have I not heeded her call?
This love radiates, burns brighter with each
diminished night, I cannot relinquish her need.
How tiring and lovely it is to fill.

CASIDA OF THE WEEPING

Katharine Rauk

for my daughter at one month, after Lorca

I listen as weeping spills from the roof
of your mouth, and swing, with you in my arms,
through every room of the house
singing. This is what it's like
to be soaked in milk. This is what it's like to want
to run out into the rain with both hands
empty. I'm done being full
like a suitcase stuffed with a river
and all its swarms of golden trout.
But the rain couldn't care less
because each second 4.4 mothers are born
while all over America radiators clang in the night
and caramel Frappuccinos are whipped into a frenzy
and 18-wheelers sail down the interstate past Tallahassee
where someone's painted the mailboxes black
Somewhere in the heartland there are warehouses stacked with
                                             paper towels
and clouds stocked with puddles
and a gardener waiting for Our Lady of Immaculate Cauliflower
to step across the mud on tiny, miraculous feet.
There's just so much to ask for: may you please
be joyful, may you taste the nip of sweetness inside a clover bud,
may you cross over the cobblestones that line Damascus Gate,
may you have a child that won't sleep
but that looks up from your breast with Gollum eyes at 3 am,
may your nipples spring leaks
and point like missiles aimed the wrong direction,
may you have as many warring tribes as ancient Rome
and fall in love and feel like an accordion
squeezed between ham-hock hands,
may you reel, may you cast a silver lure,
may you sketch the architecture of the heart a thousand times,
documenting the erasures in ink.

My greedy rosebud, my endless mouth, my immense
violin: sometimes I think I cannot love you
enough. Sometimes I want to leave you on the steps in a basket
woven from reeds
and wait for the Nile of your flooded eyes to carry you away.
Then I could be rocked by the waters of the bath
or fuck a stranger down by the lake.
Then I could wear a ball gown made of foam
or drink too many scorch-lengths of gin
or be any old squirrel I see scampering across the grass
—but then wouldn't I be crazy
for the black walnut with its inscrutable shell,
for the juice of the hull that holds the meat, that stains the
sidewalk, the patio,
that leaves the stucco of the house pockmarked with kisses
and is impossible just impossible to wash out?

INSTANTANEOUS CHANGE

Carol Dorf

No one tells a pregnant woman
what labor or the first months
will be like; that our velocity
is not continuous. The body
demands the chemical
compounds of pleasure.
As a child before gender,
I desired flight, space, rockets—
calculated trajectories and their
tangents. Later all my theories
shrunk into a particular moment—
the curve of a fretful infant
in my arms, inevitable
moment of milk's let-down.

THE LOST EDGE

Wang Ping

> *to Leo, who makes me laugh*

This is what children do:
Open the gate latches from inside
The way electricity jolts through the nerve system—
Like weeping, laughing without disguise
Like acknowledging hidden wounds.

And the things you ask shamelessly:
What makes the wind that dries the rain?
What births the stars to light our dream?
What's the pain that brings tears to the eye?
What's the eye that lifts the sun from the earth?

You make my hands tremble.

Didn't say how you conceived,
Long nights of prayers, fertility experts
From East and West.

Didn't say your body tried everything
To dispel, food, water, air. Didn't say
How bloated your limbs were, webs
Of varicose veins, stretch marks along the thighs.
Didn't say how you panted like a dog
In August heat, how food
Burned your heart with acid fire.

Didn't say. Palms on the stomach,
Tremors of a butterfly. Didn't say
How he somersaulted in the womb,
Sending tsunami waves to the liver, pancreas, heart,
How you itched from Candida,
Your nails powdery from fungi,
How your bladder lost control

Every time you sneezed or laughed.

After I scrub your broken nose,
You make me take off shoes and put down books
To chase you among trees, play hide-and-seek
You make my friends shout:
"What happened to your speed, Ping, or your brain?
Have you lost your edge since you gave birth?"

Yes, I say without apology.
When you call out for me, my four-year-old "sage,"
Your lips awash with blood and snot
When you demand my chapped hands and mouth
The way you demanded my breasts
The lock gate lifts
And the heart becomes an ocean.

At Four Years Old, What She Said to Me

Kao Kalia Yang

My daughter and I were climbing stairs.
I was pulling her along.
When she stopped, I stumbled.
She said, "You didn't let go."
I said, "I would never."
"Momma, if we die," she said,
"they will have to bury us together
because we won't stop holding hands.
They will put us in the same box.
They will put me on top of you
and I will become part of you again."

Autism Poem: The Grid

Barbara Crooker

A black and yellow spider hangs motionless in its web,
and my son, who is eleven and doesn't talk, sits
on a patch of grass by the perennial border, watching.
What does he see in his world, where geometry
is more beautiful than a human face?
Given chalk, he draws shapes on the driveway:
pentagons, hexagons, rectangles, squares.
The spider's web is a grid,
transecting the garden in equal parts.

Sometimes he stares through the mesh on a screen.
He loves things that are perforated:
toilet paper, graham crackers, coupons
in magazines, loves the order of tiny holes,
the way boundaries are defined. And real life
is messy and vague. He shrinks back to a stare,
switches off his hearing. And my heart,
not cleanly cut like a valentine, but irregular
and many-chambered, expands and contracts,
contracts and expands.

To my daughter's birth mother

Miriam Weinstein

How do I begin? Let's say I know your name. Let's say
I know where you live. Let's say, at long last I write you a letter.
Shuttled from hand to hand, weeks later, it lands on the postal
desk in the village store. I imagine you entering the open door.
Sea-green sari swaying in the breeze, curls coming loose
from your braid. The clerk looks up, mutters: *A letter for you,
Shanti.* You reach for the envelope, turn it over again and again.
Block-like shapes, swirls, and stamps cover pastel blue onionskin
paper. Let's say, an old woman watches you. Understands. *Come
with me,* she whispers, *my husband will help.* He stumbles
in the beginning, hesitates reading my letter.

How do I begin? I stumbled in the beginning. Focused
on our daughter, frequently I thought about you. Evenings,
unable to comfort her I wondered: Would swinging
in a sari-cloth hammock calm her, aroma of *channa masala*
simmering on the stove, familiar tunes of the sitar floating
in the air.

We, her mothers, remember different days. You, outside
the orphanage gate. Breasts full, arms empty. Me, across
the ocean, waiting for her to fill my empty arms.

We are linked like sand to tides.

JEREMIAH GROWING

Jenn Givhan

My son helps heal my tattoo,
scrubs his hands & under his fingernails
with antibacterial soap he'll then rub
onto the still-raw feather pen sprouting into birds

across my shoulder blade. He cups
his bicycle-calloused hands with warm
water & splashes me, losing most of the water
to the sink. Again & again he'll do this

so I'm reminded of the hotel basin I first
bathed him in, waiting for adoption papers
in an unfamiliar city, its fireflies I'd never seen,
its late-night summer sunsets. Days ago,

before the sunburn of ink
stinging my skin, he asked to meet
his birthmama, to talk to her.
It feels like I have two mamas, he said

of his heart. I texted her for permission
& she said, *I'd never say no to you—*
                He's afraid he'll wash away
my tattoo he's called beautiful, how I was afraid

as she handed him to me—*we're bound for life.*
When she called, when he saw her face
across the screen, he clutched me tighter
& asked *Mama, what should I say?*

You Were Born Early

Mary Moore Easter

for Mallory Easter Polk

We hadn't counted on you to be
the image of my father,
so recently dead,
come back as a girl,
and in miniature.
"Well, look at this Jimmy Moore!"
my mother said.

In the seventh month
days of broken water seeping out,
nights I lay still to hold you in,
to clamp you inside
just one more cycle of the moon.
We didn't know you.

In the early fear,
in the excited failure
of labor begun too soon
we didn't know you would push
your fierce way into the world,
a tiny woman howling in the birth canal
to get out and get started.

Snapshots for My Daughter

Alison Hawthorne Deming

You were five I think when we watched the cat
chase her backside under the bed
and let out a wail sharp as a bandsaw
as the first slick lump emerged.
The cord intact, she circled and circled,

and for seconds we felt the panic
she wouldn't know what to do. Then
she licked away the sac, freed the paws
to reach with inborn instructions for warmth.
You said, It wants to go back.

Nine summers later I packed you for boarding school.
You practice walk-overs in the yard, demanding,
Watch this, hey, watch! As if I could miss
the sleight of your body, breasts rising
like trick doves, the chest

I could blanket with one hand
gone for life. That summer we recovered
two iron wheels left for rubbish
by the farmer before us. We hooped them home
through the hayfield greening for a second cut

and stood them on the porch,
as if they might signify
we were ready to let go. I never felt more helpless
than when you called from Mexico, homesick,
the trip a present for your sixteenth birthday.

I gave you what you needed but I couldn't
make it easy. That night I dreamed
I carried a baby so small

the birth was painless, but the deeper rip
where the blood-lace last connected us
ached a long while into morning.

May's Scent

Kathleen Weihe

for Erin

You tell me today
it's the amygdala, emotional
memory of the brain, that helps
us identify May's scent, such
as we do: Grandma's house,
the cabin, that one resort we
stayed at where you picked
up a dead fish.

We look at your school notes,
read about the amygdala, oldest
part of the brain, time machine
for the olfactory system. More
accurate than the prime
meridian, its cells contain
the subtle knowledge of spearmint,
tomato greens, Palmolive.

I drive you to your dad's,
drop you off, and return home
again, carrying the smell
of your wet dogs, your colored
pencils, the city after rain—
wet tar, green, green evening in
May. Then, the top of your head—
rich like cut grass, only human.

Milk from Chickens

Margaret Hasse

The day my son declared with hammerhead certainty
that milk comes from chickens was the day
I yanked him out of the city
and drove west to farm and prairie land.

Like a nail pried from hard wood, he complained
from the backseat, missing electronic games and T.V.
Near the South Dakota border, he saluted
a McDonald's as we flew by.

In my country, always summer,
it is never too late to find freedom,
to open a screen door
to an entire day spent outside.

I wanted my boy to take a turn lifting barb wire
to slip into open fields
keeping an eye out for the crazy bull.
I wanted him to hold a bottle for a lamb

to feel the fierceness of animal hunger,
the suck of an animal mouth.
I wanted him to sleep out in nights encoded
with urgent messages of fireflies,

to see the bright planets in alignment overhead,
to stand on the graves of his grandparents,
dead so many years before he was born,
and to trace the names etched on granite pillows,

hard as the last sleep.
How else to plant in him the long root of plains grass,
help him reach water in drought and
know who his family is?

To My Son Upon His First Visit to Lebanon

Hedy Habra

He wanted to see our summerhouse
    in the mountains of Baabdat,
enter the pictures
        where a young woman his age,
    her long hair flowing in the wind,
guided his first steps on the terrace of the villa.
He wanted to dream in a language never learned,
    see himself reflected in familiar faces,
recapture smells and fragrances.

He finally saw the orchard his father planted
    tree after tree, green and black figs, cherries,
peaches, plums, pears, apples and almonds . . .
        One hundred fruit trees
    we would not see blossoming
        spring after spring.
    And the purple grape seeds from Japan,
the miniature green seedless *Banati* from Egypt,
    covering the trellis, tempting clusters hanging low,
casting shadows on the shaded patio.

The cut stone house with its tiled roof
    seemed out of place.
What ever happened
    to the one in the family album?
No longer surrounded by green mountain slopes,
nor an open view to the horizon.
    Erratic buildings sprouted like mushrooms
during the civil war.
Concrete was biting the flanks of the mountains,
    spreading like a contagious disease.

He rang the doorbell.

The tenants were friendly, inviting him in.
   They said the present owner was very proud
of his orchard, that he himself
    had planted each one of these tall, imposing trees . . .
He called us excited, said he wanted to buy
the house back. We could spend summers there.
Time regained, he thought,
    eager to relive our dream,
retrieve its lost broken pieces,

I tried to explain what does belonging *mean* exactly?
And does it really matter?

Conspiracy

Camille T. Dungy

> *to breathe together*

Last week, a woman smiled at my daughter and I wondered
if she might have been the sort of girl my mother says spat on my aunt
when they were children in Virginia all those acts and laws ago.

Half the time I can't tell my experiences apart from the ghosts'.

A shirt my mother gave me settles into my chest.

I should say *onto my chest*, but I am self conscious—
the way the men watch me while I move toward them
makes my heart trip and slide and threaten to bruise
so that, inside my chest, I feel the pressure of her body,
her mother's breasts, her mother's mother's big, loving bounty.

I wear my daughter the way some women other places are taught
to wear their young. Sometimes, when people smile,
I wonder if they think I am being quaintly primitive.

The cloth I wrap her in is brightly patterned, African,
and the baby's hair manes her alert head in such a way
she has often been compared to an animal.

There is a stroller in the garage, but I don't want to be taken
as my own child's nanny. (Half the time I know my fears are mine
                                                                    alone.)

At my shower, a Cameroonian woman helped me practice
putting a toy baby on my back. I stood in the middle of a circle
of women, stooped over and fumbling with the cloth. Curious
                                                                    George
was the only doll on hand, so the white women looked away
afraid I would hurt my baby while the black women looked away
and thought about not thinking about monkeys.

I walk everyday with my daughter and wonder
what is happening to other people's minds. Half the time
I am filled with terror. Half the time I am full of myself.

The baby is sleeping on my back again. When I stand still,
I can feel her breathing. But when I start to move, I lose her
in the rhythms of my tread.

Jennifer's Kitchen

Toni Easterson

We sat at a table in Jennifer's kitchen,
you and I, Sarah and sometimes Polly,
on the periphery of a still life:
mugs of tea, apple slices, a plate of cookies,
an Evenflo bottle and shards of graham crackers.
There was always a baby pulling herself up
to a wobbly stance against one of our knees,
our toddlers played with toys in the living room.

I don't remember what we talked about but
maybe you do. I remember only the burlap
curtains at the windows and the fragile lifelines
we tossed across the table to each other.

Lost Mothers

Kimberly Blaeser

Our own gone the way of aprons
the way of ritual Saturday cleanings—
every head pink with a mass of sponge curlers
or demur beneath a flowered headscarf.

Are our children's mothers likewise obsolete?

The handy craft cabinet still jammed:
stamp pads and hole punchers patient
amid construction paper and finger paints—
but chubby hands we guided now grown.

Will motherhood transform, follow us to Social Security?

Yes, texting and Facebook learned from our "babies;"
our favorite slippers older than the new podiatrist,
now we give applause instead of allowance,
our hands hold cell phones as we cross busy decades—

look both ways, pray tradition becomes retro enough to appeal.

Now we share space with "heirloom" birchbark baskets,
patchwork quilts and embroidered tablecloths, with women's
stories—we tell the simple eloquence of enduring,
of mothers making beauty with the bent and broken.

Those lost hands reappear in feverish dreams, shadows of our dailiness.

Pain too, a legacy we inherit from an era of disposable
women—courtier or courtesan in the castles of men.
Their dutiful service fired in us a restless independence,
working mothers claiming diplomas, careers—and solidarity.

The holy mantle of leadership is a mother's grace.

As Morning Fingers off the Glove of Night

Elizabeth Weir

I see three plump shapes huddled
on a log of silver maple, silhouetted
against a wind-scuffed lake.

The sun slips free of the horizon
and they're Canada geese,
shrugged-up against early spring cold.

The middle bird has drooping wings,
one more dropped than the other.
Injured, I assume—won't do well.

Hours later, I check again,
and two birds have left the log
to forage close by.

The middle bird stands, stretches
wings and reveals three pairs
of spiky legs—week-old goslings.

Night-long she has sheltered them
in the warm muff of her wings—I feel
instant kinship, know her need to nurture.

MOTHER'S DAY

Norita Dittberner-Jax

On Mother's Day Sunday,
I walk with my family
to the ice cream store, the first
cones of the season, ten of us,
walking the neighborhood.

The wheels of the stroller
hit me in the heels once or twice,
as we pass through a corridor
of trees just greening and the first
bush to flower, the yellow forsythia.

They give me cards with arrows
of love in handwriting I would know
anywhere. The daughter missing is not
really missing. She sends a message
from Duluth that zings my heart
with an IOU for ice cream later.

When they leave and the afternoon
collapses into quiet after the ruckus,
I read the newspaper. Behind the headlines,
a Million Mothers are marching in Washington
against the gunfire that killed their children.

Our Lady of Rocamadour

Mary Kay Rummel

Shrine in Southwestern France

I've climbed these two hundred steps,
not on my knees as medieval penitents,
but on my own sore feet, bunions and hammer toes.
In the twelfth century chapel, she waits,
the black Madonna in a red glow
where she's brooded over centuries of pilgrims
scallop shells pinned to their breasts.
She's serene, shining in her ebony wood,
a dark star.

Holding her small son, she reigns
over the long history of love and loss.
I pray for my two sons trudging the maze
of their middle years,
I'm falling behind them.
Ahead of us their shining daughters,
long hair blowing, want to fly.

I don't expect this Dark Mother
to save us, but I believe in ritual—
believe in being born a second time.
I keep walking even though it hurts, one foot
in front of the other on this stony climb.
Below the parapets hawks soar on thermals,
bright wings keeping them aloft
on tides of air, imperceptible
as gravity or light.

PRAYER

Ann Fisher-Wirth

Let the mothers rush toward their babies
and wrap their arms around them tight enough
to hold back even the sea if it would harm them.

Let the anguish melt from the fathers' eyes.
This summer, the birds are going crazy with melody
in the jungle of wisteria and privet

that shelters my house, and at dawn the air
is fresh—there is sweetness in my life.
One Christmas Eve when our five were small

they asked to sleep on pallets so they could
be near the tree, these children of divorce
who came and went, who were apart from me

for months at a time. I sneaked into the room
just to be near the beloved tumble of arms
and legs, just to hear them breathe. That

bodily adoration. One whispered in her sleep,
one held her brother's toe, and the tree
with its shadowy packages loomed over them

in the dark, lit by a slant of light through the door.
When I first learned about war, I would
lie in bed brute with horror that a man

could tear a baby from its mother's arms.
That a man could *choose* to tear a baby
from its mother's arms. But so we see it now, each day.

Between the Ceiling & the Moon

Deborah Cooper

My mother's hand
miscalculates her mouth.
She keeps jabbing the cookie
into her chin.
"Are my teeth in?" she asks,
as if this might be the problem.

Last week she told me
she'd been stuck up
on the ceiling
for the longest time.
Today I hang a string
of tinfoil stars
above her bed.

The circumference of her life
is pulled tighter
with each round of the clock,
like a knot, like a seed
that will break open elsewhere.

And still, she asks
each time I walk into her room
"Has the baby come yet?"
and something loosens in my chest.
My daughter is serene and round
and luminous,
as if she had swallowed the moon.

Now the moon
is following me home,
the new moon,
holding the shadow

of the old;
the old moon,
graciously giving itself up.

THE VIOLETS

Sanjana Nair

Of course the violets slay me

with their perfect tiny bodies, their winking eyes
blinking a fierce kind of joy in the shadow of the pines, still

green after a bitter winter. The wood—
piled so high, it seems certain that warmth will
happen. The snow has other ideas. We resort to bodies:

The way we survive. What are we two
in the land's realm, her weathered defense
against the dark hungers and silly thirsts of man,
the constant excavation of her bones and deep secrets and watery veins.

The body of a mother blooms and I'm full
of another's DNA, the wilderness of another's eyes,
her little lungs, the perfect pair of kidneys and the hungry belly,
linked to my own belly. She will become heiress to the pain that has razed
a planet's existence, always female—her disappeared rail birds come
                                        back, the coelacanth

returned amongst the sunken remains
of Hanuman's drowned bridge. The breathing
found in distant India. In my belly. On the other's
shores—how I miss the sometimes trees. The green and blue of them,
the way history is colored *elsewhere*. In this America, non-birth is
                                        being named
murder; the girls are endangered. Here, we sit mute and watch in
                                        horror at anything

we can name *other*. Isn't woman
a reason to live? Let daughters be born into fields
of wild violets where they are adored. Let daughters know

they are not done in by the Technicolor fans of their delicate bodies.
What good is the shore without their hands digging through sand
                                              collecting the shells—
What good are the woods without their hands digging into the
                                    dirt, foraging delicate fungi—
What good are we, if we don't put our arms around the girls,
around the women who make them—

Covalent Bonds

Gwen Nell Westerman

we are
        dream carriers
child bearers
those burdens borne
with hope
and intensity
under the gravity
of responsibility
history and
love
not guilt
love
and hope
for those who
will dream
and share
these burdens born
we do not give up
willingly
        but attract and repel
balance and share
stronger
in that bond of
love

Tell Me of This Parting

TABLE TALK

Carol Masters

You and your boys knelt easily,
rapt at the ragged march of ants
across a stone, thread of light sliding
like a river, the sun stretching
on and on, all of you could wait.

How did it happen?

How did their fair unfolding
so dazzle you that they've grown and gone
while yours and the earth's years sped past?

You thought you would give them the world.

PARTING

Florence Chard Dacey

I crave no more babies,
I say, sucking on the lie,
swaggering off to write.
My back is stiff from birthing.
I am overqualified for this job.
Mouthing it like a toddler,

Mother.

I'm nurturing art.
No more fingering booties in the attic.
No more flipping whole-wheat pancakes.
This last child may cry,
but she'll outlive me
just as I rehearse to outlive,

Mother, you.

You carried five of us, all grown now.
Yet you are still putting up love
in your kitchen on August nights.
Can't let it go to waste. Mother-love,
the vine we prune back, but won't uproot.
We think we won't survive the cutting.

Mother, you did.

A mother does, makes loss a religion.
Watches her body walk away
without a backward glance,
serrated into two or six or ten.
That, or straps the children to her
till she is one misshapen lumbering beast,

hacking at herself in vain, but

Mother, you did not.

Or live as if you didn't.
Don't pry or whine. Keep your calculated distance,
like this I calculate and cultivate.
Is it anything but shield
against that truth,

Mother, you did not tell me.

That we must let life and death
flow out of us in them,
know they know to hold them
is to kill, to let them go is too,
and that our daughters will return to say

Mother, you did not tell me of this.

You did not tell me I would have to breathe lies:
You'll be fine, I'll be back soon.
You did not tell me of this flesh
that would sprout in mine like wheat,
this flesh I fatten for the scythe.
You did not tell me I would be
both flesh and scythe.

Oh, Mother, you did not tell me of this parting.

CAESAREAN BIRTH, MID-TWENTIETH CENTURY

Florence Weinberger

The cut to Aurelia, mother of Caesar, was only myth,
      but, my impeccable first daughter, I was
sliced open, and you were ripped out pink and bawling,
      to save us both.

Someone showed me toenails, too swift to take in,
then whisked you away,
would not let me claim you nine heartsick days. Some rumor
of contagion afflicting the corridors.

      They taught me sneaking.
I soft-slippered down to the nursery window; I think I waved
      but the doctors held sway,
slipped pills into my food, the way they do with prisoners.

      They dried my milk.
How do I swathe you in lost time? Every night you call
      around eleven. For uncounted minutes,
we talk about our fevers.

EXILE

Alicia Suskin Ostriker

The downward turning touch
the cry of time
fire falling without sound
plunge my hand in the wound

children marching and dying
all that I do is a crime
because I do not reach
their mouths silently crying

my boychild reaches with his mouth
it is easy, being a mother
his skin is tender and soft
kisses stitch us together

we love as long as we may
then come years without kisses
when he will turn away
not to waste breath

when I too will fall
embracing a pillow at night
touching the stone of exile
reaching my hand to death

during the evacuation of Phnom Penh, 1975

They Slip Away

Edith Rylander

Nights when the news is bad
(Catastrophes and corpses,
Guns and the usual lies)
I dream I am holding a baby.

Not any particular child;
Not mine, nor my new granddaughter.
No little face I know.
But dreaming arms remember

The heft of small weight,
The warm, milk-smelling morsel
Of some wobbly-headed newborn
Nuzzling against my chest.

The butt fits in my palm.
The miniature fingers
Clasp my big hand;
I know every bone by feel,

Know the pulse at the fontanelles
Where the skull plates have not yet fused
Over the forming mind
In its small breakable case.

Always they slip away,
No matter how tight I hold them.
They leap from my arms like fish,
Or frogs, or excited kittens.

I never let them fall.
I guard them every second
With the tightest clutch I know,

But they squirt like melon seeds

Out of my best protection,
Going wherever they go,
Leaving me clutching emptiness.
Always, they slip away.

LONG DISTANCE

Ethna McKiernan

Time rushes backward through the wires—
their voices on the phone tonight small
as early childhood, reeling me back
to Naoise with peas stuck in his ears, to Conor
in that store hissing to the kind clerk
that God gave him that truck,
so bug off. Hanging up, I thought of the kid
this morning doing handstands
on the lawn, how I wanted to grab the bright coin
of him and squander its riches all on me
until love and poverty were the only things left.

We always want what's leaving us:
our sons like meteors, speeding away
from us toward adolescence;
that moment in October when light
charges leaves and limbs equally
and then vanishes; the song
whose words slip away in sleep,
troubling our morning coffee.

Talk to me, babies, rub the ocean's joy
into the mouthpiece until I feel the salt
on your lips as you answer me
in monosyllables, *nope, yep, 'K, bye,*
holding back the thing
you don't know how to give.

That and Not

Mary Kay Rummel

In two hours the fog-bound night heron
has not moved from the neighbor's roof,
its snake neck and beak stretched
as if fishing in air,
each mottled feather visible
on a tweedy breast facing north.

Could be a kind of goodbye
the same as I feel these days.
Could be blessing the house
where a young couple wait
for a child to arrive.

Could be trying to see its own brightness
the way a mother studies her child,
the angel's awed-by-her-beauty look
in Donatello's annunciation,
all surprised tenderness, the virgin.

Could be wanting a message
like the call from my son in L.A.
After filming a birth he wants to thank me
for having him, calls me a perfect parent,
but I know the failures, I count them
leaf by plunging leaf.

Here where the cold wind sends birds
hurling themselves over lakes
in long strings of sentences,
the heron has waited too long.
Stay, risk the cold, I want to say
but I can't promise anything, not even
attention enough

to keep the grey body from lifting
into a sky, suddenly bereft.

Michaelangelo saw the end of it,
as his pietá arose from stone.
He carved that pain into the mother's face.

IN A LAND WHERE EVERYTHING IS ALREADY TRYING TO KILL ME, I ENTER A NEW PHASE OF MY LIFE IN WHICH IT WOULD BE VERY BAD IF I DIED

Claire Wahmanholm

because now there is a child and its mother is burning
with rapture and terror and has my eyes and teeth.
She is parasite, doppelganger, and I would die
if she unmothered me. She holds my breath as I pass
a speeding truck. She holds my breath when we see
a mother duck and a duckling that would not know
if she died. We are not that kind. Our kind keens
for a long time and the sadness accumulates in our bodies
like lead or tapeworm eggs. I feel sorry for all of us,
the leaving and the left. Everything is bearing down,
bearing down. For "bereft," make a tearing sound,
which is different from a tearing sound, which is made
behind the face instead of at the base of the throat.
I hold my breath so I can't choke to death. A child
watches me not eat my sandwich. It is my child,
it is my own watchfulness, we are the same kind,
the sandwich is stale, we stare at it balefully.
It would be kind of the world to let us live until
we are tired of it, until it is stale and unpleasurable.
But that is called *heaven*, not *world*. Once I am dead,
I won't know it, but that doesn't help. I already miss living—
all its bells and tulips and feelings. There is *maybe* death
and there is *death* death and that's all. I will spend
the rest of my life maybe dying until I actually do.
I have practiced and practiced. I have tried to drive out
the sugar that attracts the sadness. But the mother in me
has fallen in love with everything. I want to tell her
to shut her eyes, to keep her hands in her pockets,
but she must hold the child's hand as she crosses the street.
She must eat if she wants to see the child, which is better
than eating. I have not left her any white stones
to follow out of this forest. There is only the sweet
dangerous darkness and the fire at the end of it.

Tidal Wave

Freya Manfred

How will I swim
with both arms
holding twin sons?

Should I save
the soft-hearted boy
born with one raised fist?

Or the boy
who first saw the stars
beyond my face?

Over and over
I choose them both,
stroking toward the light.

Why do I feel satisfied
riding the curve of my death
and theirs?

I am doing what I can
even if it is never
enough.

Perseids

Rebecca Foust

When the real star died and fell, I knew the others for tricks,
trompe d'oeil on insides of eyelids. But it was no trick
when that star larger than sky fell out of my sky,

shock of arc-then-black. My son has chest pains again. *I thought
we were past this.* When he was a child it was easy to hold
his hand all night so he wouldn't die—

trace toxins in cereal, the new mole on his left little toe—I sang
him back to sleep and the next day he was off again,
climbing trees higher than I could reach

or hunching all day over a fixed lens, knotting a fish line fine
as an eyelash. He collects horseshoe crab trash,
knowing and naming each slender spire—

I broke one once and hid the pieces, but he missed it later,
back to sing to his darlings, constelled in precise
patterns in the sky of his bedroom floor.

He's tall now, with a beard. The astral map is in pieces,
just as real stars come unmoored and fall
into flaming comets. Power fails,

EKGs skip and stutter, MRIs hum, then blink off. Boys
he knew in school come home from Iraq without legs.
He trolls the internet for side effects

of medicine he takes to decrease the world's discomfort
with him. "Rarely fatal" *doesn't mean never,*
and what logic doesn't whet each day's edge

with fear? *I could die, I might die, we all die. I'll die.*
Maybe tonight, alone in his sleep. *Don't get mad,*
Mom. We've done all the tests twice,

but being alive means proving a negative. So how
can we go on believing each day won't be the one
that flames out? When he walks in his sleep,

his eyes are open and dark, night-terror pools. Shh, now
he's dropping off, worry lines etching his forehead,
shape of his mouth sucked into the neck

of his tee shirt. Overhead, stars arc across the dark sky
making small curved rips, and the light leaks out.

The Wailing Room

Allison Adelle Hedge Coke

Always, when it seems just fine,
something stirs against living
steals those we least expect
sometimes murders
comes in fours
fully cornered, squared,
unnaturally man-made tight.

Creeps along skull hunting,
especially those who come with criers
wildly wailing their loss
in deathwatch chambers.
Quiet now, children. Quiet now.

All our grandparents, uncles,
most aunties, some cousins, three brothers—
before they'd even crawled—
friends, some of their kids, brothers,
my one song man—all gone.

Last to go my daughter-in-law's father,
only a few days younger than me he was.
Strong as a bull bear, least what we thought.
Gone, gone.

Both her grandmas,
only grandpa she ever knew,
all gone in a short time.
Gone, gone, gone, she's crying.

My girl, I wish you long life.
Quiet now, they'll hear you.
Some of us see them walking in day,

more at night,   all hesitate knowing
what surrounds us here.
Up to the deathbed, Ravenmocking.
Outside the wailing room, all of you—
Quiet now, children.   Quiet now.

FEBRUARY SECOND

Barbara Crooker

The snow is coming down again, the ground pale as Snow White's skin,
and a blood-red cardinal lands on the black lid of the barbecue,
where I've scattered some seeds. In the book I'm reading, a sentence
flies off the page, flaps between my eyes: *It's a happy life, but someone
is missing.* Someone is always missing. Time stopped forty years ago
in the delivery room in those last moments before the nurse
couldn't find the heartbeat. I became a watch that no longer ticks.
You cannot change time, but I wish I could be innocent again,
believing all stories have happy endings. *Closure is bullshit.*
You never forget, though everyone else does. Here is a birthday
unmarked on a calendar, where no cake is baked, no icing piles up
in drifts, no candles are wished on. Forever after, I am the bad fairy,
the one you don't want to invite to the christening. This story is
so sad that no one remembers it, and I have to tell it again and again.
Just like this snow, which keeps stuttering down, trying to write
its little white lies, but the black facts refuse to be swaddled;
their harsh calls rise up, crows on the snow.

Lines in italics are from An Exact Replica of a Figment
of My Imagination *by Elizabeth McCracken. A child dies
in this book.... a baby is stillborn.*

Elegy for a Daughter

Jeanne Lutz

Here at the hospital I rub
her foldy, bold skin. She
weighs three point two pounds.
I rub her arms, her legs,
and her back. I tell her stories,
watch her breathe, her baggy
face changing expressions
as if she's rehearsing
future emotions. Experts
say caressing preemie babies
improves nearly everything
by eighty percent,
or something like that.
They gain weight, wit,
smarts, and immunities,
a talent for happiness,
compassion, and cooking,
being a good leader,
and if not that, then knowing
who to follow. I won't say
any of this in the past tense—
that's not where hope
should be. Soon she'll know
what sun and wind
and rain feel like. Falling
in love will be sweet. Staying
in love, even sweeter.
She'll grow into this skin
and it will stay, I swear,
as thick as it ever was,
or needs to be, and words
will never hurt her.

The Pietá Is Featured on Yet Another Website for Bereaved Moms

Sue Reed Crouse

There's Mary again, Mother of God, holding the dead
Christ, her grief agleam and bowed beauty intact.

The way her raiment gathers so delicately
over her forehead is enough to make me doubt.

Some of us identify with another Mary, mother
of dead Willie and dead Tad, with her hysterics and wild hair.

Even Abe called her *Mother*, until the day he was murdered
in the theater. Now *she's* a mother with whom to wail.

I summon her like she called her dead, and together
we'll buy hundreds of hats that we'll stack in unused rooms.

We'll interview mediums until we can find one who can shake
the table and whip the ether into stiff peaks.

We'll bid on armoires and ball gowns. We'll hold
one another. We'll laugh and keen with the same screech.

Mary Todd, I love your rough chapped cheeks, upended
brilliance, and the way you kept your pain stripped and shaking.

The lustrous Mary's son was back from the dead before her mind
had time to untwine itself. Oh Mary Todd, our kids stayed dead.

Mary, you are my pietá, wailing for Willie, for Abe and for Tad,
you, hot-faced on the floor, in the crumpled pile of your stiff dress.

The Shadow Child

Elizabeth Oness

You would have been born twenty years ago today—

Girl-child, solstice baby, I'd allowed myself to choose
Tiny clothes with shining stars.

You're eclipsed by your brother, who is almost
The age of your father when we met.

You were named, expected as the sunlight.
When asked if I have children, I sometimes answer
In the plural, as you are present in your absence.

TALKING WITH MY DEAD DAUGHTER

Jo McDougall

1

Today I read of an artist who uses dust
from the homes of her subjects
to paint their portraits,
mixing it with bright oils.

Why did I not think of this?
Dust from your grave
so bright and powdery
it would warble like sunlit mica

as I smeared the canvas with my hands,
tracing your bones and smile and body,
the pandemonium of your hair.

2

Why do my words fall apart
whenever I describe you?

I was the one Fate chose
to keep you alive, to make the air
remember.
Now and then—minutes, seconds go by—
I don't think of you.
I've failed at grief.

MISCARRIAGE INTERPRETED THROUGH ANIMAL SCIENCE

Jenn Givhan

After mating & laying her eggs,
the octopus with a brain the size of a clementine

goes senile. She welds herself into
a cracked teapot she'd grown fond of

then dries up. Researchers find her yards from her tank
finally still after days of odd behavior.

What size was her heart?
That's not what we mean of course but the neurons

in her arms as if each had its own brain—
when cut, will regrow. When cut,

will continue searching for food then surrender
prey to mouth as if the mouth were still attached

& still I lie on my side instead of my belly, pillow
between my legs. This is more than phantom limb

as the octopus must know.

What is it like to be an octopus?

What I'm asking is how we carry on.

All the Words by Heart

I Write My Son's Birth

Jennifer Manthey

> *After a mother at a friend's birthday party lights her*
> *child's candles at the exact minute he was born, and*
> *my adopted child asks me, "What time was I born?"*

There was the waxed and colorful dress she wore to meet
you. Outside: the unrealized river, fantasy of jungle, whole
economy of rain.

There was notable heat, of course, humid steady breath.
The moringa reached its branches, gathered as much sky
as it could.

She cleaned her kitchen for your coming. Pots shined.
Spoons held each other at sounds of her pain. Knives
stood brave.

Impala leaped, stood on two legs; their horns blessed the
doorway. Lions came, gave their voice to you, left with
tails swishing.

She knew the earth beneath her. Unmoved.
Dust stirred toward bones. Blood-fight of her
body.

There is a way a woman is washed with
birth. Calm devotion. Not-miracle.

And Shala, like I said at the party, it was six a.m.
Early morning, new as you in the constant
equatorial sun.

WANT

Jessica Fisher

As she nurses, my nipple takes on the color of her lips. This is the definition of love: to become indistinguishable. She was me, then mine; now wherever I go she follows. But which "e" is lost when *where* and *ever* meet? We went looking, though we knew we wouldn't find it. High & Low a fool's game. The contraction came into play because we need less than is sometimes given; it's a gesture to try to make what's written match what's said. They started at two minutes apart. *What's your date of birth* became a confusing question, as did the verb *deliver.* Did I, or was I? She was born of our love, to which we signed our names. A wanted child, crying I want you in the night. *Then want must be your master.* Hidden in the annals, the etymologist found, is another meaning, now housed in the English Dialect Dictionary. A want furrows. Why outfox it? Condensation on the window or in the mind indicates you're not where you thought. He was very handsome and had a bricklayer's hands, though he worked in concrete. He explained the logic of the contraction joint as we waited for the bus: you have to build in a break, because it grows.

The Waiting

Iris Jamahl Dunkle

for Jackson

Once you arrived we walked the block like convicts:
you, a tiny bundle in a green felt snowsuit,
me, wearing a body too large to recognize as my own.

The leaves chattered their teeth, the wind shoved us along.
We hadn't found words yet. We spoke in touch.

I point out the monuments of our walk:
Snow White and the Seven Dwarves figurines
tucked behind an abandoned house.
Winter apple trees clinging to their red, shriveled fruit.
The path out—

But, always we'd return to the white shuttered house,
to the unbundling, to the flush of warm air awakening our faces.

And each day words formed and you spoke to me:
stones dropped in an ink-dark pool.

Writing About the First Months

Carolyn Williams-Noren

No adjective changes baby.
Baby is butter. Baby is sugar.
Baby talks to the deep mammal brain.

Trouble is baby
reads like *sweet*. Put baby down
and loveliness looms up.

I am miserable
taking care
of this baby. Miserable

is the stinger of a honeybee
licking the sticky stamen
of the six-foot hollyhock of *baby*.

Try it. Say *I'm so tired*
of this baby. Baby is hungry. Baby
swallows every other word

mashed and strained.

HUNGER

Marianne Murphy Zarzana

Oh, those milky orbs, so useful in their beauty, so beautiful
in their usefulness, those gorgeous jugs with their ability
to satiate both baby and lover, day and night, even as I moved
behind a veil of fatigue and hunger, snuck naps, gobbled
peanut butter sandwiches, guzzled beer for extra protein.
My only goal—maximize production, bind body and soul,
this body, this first book my daughter read with her lips.

I miss those breasts, brimful of milk, and so does my husband,
so we tell stories to bring them back for brief appearances.
He recounts his emergency stash of baby formula, bottles nestled
into socks like small creatures burrowed deep into his bottom drawer.
I'd mandated a ban, a prohibition on all such bottles. *My* baby's lips
would suckle only from *my* nipples, drink only *my* milk, but this
ravenous baby girl never left any excess to pump, freeze in the fridge.
When I believed her belly full enough that I could dash off for lunch
with a friend, leave her with her daddy, later he'd tell me how soon
she cried, inconsolable. His contraband discovered, I conceded.

At 21, our daughter carries her breasts well, holds them high, open
to a hard world, holds them against me when I hug her, sweaty,
after she's told me the story of her tough workday at summer camp,
not the kids she loves, has learned how to wrangle, not the ticks
she plucks off, the price she'll pay to feed her hunger for earth, tree,
rock, and stream, but the too-muchness of it all. I press her body
against mine as it quakes into quiet sobs. Her tears no longer release
milk from my breasts, but I do what I can. I hold her in my arms,
in these words.

INSIDE

Riki Kölbl Nelson

for Benno

Nuzzle, cuddle, babble
say all the sweet words
you want
silly, selig nonsense

hum the faint song
your bones knew
forming slowly
in the womb

recall the inside curve
the ever present drum
the red cradle
rocking
day after day

Sailor Mom

Carol Kapaun Ratchenski

I swore at my babies. Like a sailor-mom. It is not the parenting
behavior I am proudest of, but my sisters will tell you if I don't.
I walked them in the middle of the night, teething or fevering
with earaches and in the sweetest most nurturing voice you could
imagine I swore at my babies. It helped me and they were pre-
language, aware only of tone and touch. I was gentle at both and
profane. Even after his diagnosis, I didn't stop though I tried then
because I was ashamed and thought his illness might even be the
result of such harsh words in his tender membrane ears. If in the
new age I am responsible for my reality then surely my foul mouth
could have grown black tumor cells in his brain. At four in the
morning this made sense and I swore anyway. Too tired to censor,
craving sleep more than long life for either of us. Medicine to give
every two hours, portable IV hydration, a grotesque backpack
for toddlers needing round-the-clock chemotherapy drugs, new
obscenities every day. Swearing helped; red wine and a pinch or
two of his medical marijuana over my oatmeal. I don't apologize.
Fuck the new age.

BEFORE LANGUAGE

Karen Herseth Wee

Daughter, sometimes I know your eyes follow
me and I would like to talk
to you in the language of women
easy in each other's company

So often when I try the words are wrong
My humor like a tune off-key
not well-received in your ear or your heart
But I promise you I'll wait for a day

when we reach the same language
the sounds deep in our memories
of another time when in the womb
strumming the same chord we needed no words

MOTHER DAUGHTER HOUR

Camille T. Dungy

    Callie is reading the book about language,
and I am reading the book about death.

Ball, she says, pointing to an orange.
        I shake my head.

        I read, *Death is the mother of beauty.*
   She says, *pretty ball.*

I am going to have to put down my book so I can teach her better,
       but first I read her one last sentence
       because I am struck by all its vowel sounds.

        That, finally, is all it means
  to be alive: to be able to die.

       She is listening
and she is not listening.

The afternoon light is brighter here on the couch than any other place
      in the room.

    With her little thumb and baby fingers, my daughter turns
      her board book's pages.
                Red, she says,
    pointing to an apple.

Red, I say, and we sit together a while longer. Read some more.

WHEREAS STATEMENT [13]

Layli Long Soldier

WHEREAS her birth signaled the responsibility as mother to teach what it is to be Lakota, therein the question: what did I know about being Lakota? Signaled panic, blood rush my embarrassment. What did I know of our language but pieces? Would I teach her to be pieces. Until a friend comforted, *don't worry, you and your daughter will learn together.* Today she stood sunlight on her shoulders lean and straight to share a song in Diné, her father's language. To sing she motions simultaneously with her hands. I watch her be in multiple musics. At a ceremony

to honor the Diné Nation's first poet laureate, a speaker explains that each People has been given their own language to reach with. I understand reaching as active, a motion. He offers a prayer and introduction in heritage language. I listen as I reach my eyes into my hands, my hands onto my lap, my lap as the quiet page I hold my daughter in. I rock her back, forward, to the rise of other conversations

about mother tongues versus foster languages, belonging. I connect the dots. I rock in time with references to a philosopher, a master language-thinker who thought of his mother too. Mother-to-child and child-to-mother relationships. But as this philosopher's mother suffered the ill-effects of a stroke he wrote, *I asked her if she was in pain (yes) then where? [. . . she] replies to my question: I have a pain in my mother, as though she were speaking for me, both in my direction and in my place.* His mother, who spoke in his place for his pain and as herself for her own, did this as one-and-the-same. Yet he would propose understanding the wor*d mother* by what mother is not, the *différance.* Forward, back. I lift my feet

my toes touch ground as I'm reminded of the linguistic impossibility of identity, as if any of us can be identical ever. To whom, to what? Perhaps to Not. I hold my daughter in comfort saying *iyotanchilah michuwintku.* True, I'm never sure how to write our language on the page correctly, the written takes many forms

yet I know she understands through our motion. Rocking, in this country of so many languages where national surveys assert that Native languages are dying. Child-speakers and elder teachers dwindle, this is public information. But her father and I don't teach in statistics, in this dying I mean. Whereas speaking, itself, is *defiance*—the closest I can come to *différance.* Whereas I confess

these are numbered hours spent responding to a national apology which concerns us, my family. These hours alone to think, without. My hope: my daughter understands wholeness for what it is, not for what it's not, all of it the pieces;

NAMING MY DAUGHTER

Patricia Fargnoli

The one who took hold in the cold night
The one who kicked loudly
The one who slid down quickly in the ice storm
She who came while the doctor was eating dessert
New one held up by heels in the glare
The river between two brothers
Second pot on the stove
Princess of a hundred dolls
Hair like water falling beneath moonlight
Strides into the day
She who runs away with motorcycle club president
Daughter kicked with a boot
Daughter blizzard in the sky
Daughter night-pocket
She who sells sports club memberships
One who loves over and over
She who wants child but lost one
She who wants marriage but has none
She who never gives up
Diana (Goddess of the Chase)
Doris (for the carrot-top grandmother
she never knew)
Fargnoli (for the father
who drank and left and died)
Peter Pan, Iron Pumper
Tumbleweed who goes months without calling
Daughter who is a pillar of light
Daughter mirror. Daughter stands alone
Daughter boomerang who always comes back
Daughter who flies forward into the day
where I will be nameless.

Post-Adoption, The Naming

Paige Riehl

I.

Girl of so many names,
written horizontally and vertically,

rearranged
by trembling hands.

Each is a truth,
a blanket to wrap
        or fling into the fire.

II.

We wish no harm—
we as (birth) Mother, (foster) Mother,
(adoptive) Mother.

We separated
        by black oceans and wrinkled calendars.

We weighted
        by our labels, such heavy coats.

We wish
        you the past as a compass,

wish you today
as a curtain
opening,

wish you decades in sprawling cities
in languages,
in moonlight, in oceans.

III.

Three mothers' arms
like flowering pears.
There are so many ways
to view this—
        but who am I to say?

I've heard the fury from others—
        infertile white bitch—

Yet, I come from the place
where it is easiest to be happy.

IV.

In ten years. Twenty.
Perhaps contented afternoons.
Perhaps slammed doors,
the voice like a hammer.

Words. Lightning bolts
in a drought. I will offer you water
from my cupped hands.

YES

Carrie Fountain

I am done smoking cigarettes, done waiting tables, done counting tips
at two a.m. in the neon-dark dance hall, done sleeping with young men
in my apartment, done facing them or not, thinking of oblivion, which
is better than nothing. I am done not wearing underwear because
it's so Victorian. I am done telling men I don't wear underwear because
it's so Victorian. I am done with the night a guy spread my legs
on a pool table, all those balls piled up in the pockets. I am done.
I am never going back. When I see that night on the street I will
drive past and never even glance over. I am done going to grad school,
nodding in your workshop. I am done teaching English as a second
language, saying *I* pointing to my chest, saying *you* pointing to them.
I am done teaching the poetry class where no one talked and no one
listened to me and outside the window the cottonwood wagged
its sun-white leaves in the breeze as if to say, *I give up, I give up.* I am done
being a childless woman, a childless wife, a woman with no scars
on her body. I am done with the wide afternoons of before, the long
stare, the tightly closed door. And I am done, too, for the most part,
with the daydream of after. I am after for now. I am turning up the heater
to see if that will make the baby sleep another fifteen minutes
so I can finish this poem. I am done thinking of the past as if it had
survived, though sometimes I think of the past and sometimes I see it
coming, catching up, hands caked with dried mud, head shaved clean.

STILL LIFE WITH PEEVED MADONNA

Adrian Blevins

It's clear I'm standing on the Isle of Motherdom
given these three children hanging off my arms and feet

weighing the weight of the planet, at least.
The children look like dime-store bric-a-brac

since all that swings will squarely star-sparkle,
but more like missiles in size and expulsion interest.

They're asking how cold is the water, to which I say I don't know.
They're asking could they have some macaroni & cheese

to which I say I'm occupied hating this line, hush, now hush.
They're asking how far it is inland & do the natives dance there

& can they go & get some confetti & snort or inject it
to which I say years ago I could answer your questions

but look at those clouds, I think that's a cyclone
to which they say, fuck you, Mom, you're always so paranoid

to which I say, fuck you, too, you remind me of lizards,
were you birthed in an outhouse by an ogre or a loon?

LETTER TO THE FIRST BORN

Edith Rylander

Kept dreaming about you all night long,
Every dream more depressing than the last,
Though in the dreams, at least you were coming home
Like you used to. Old wreck cars rumbling
Into the driveway, you
Skinny as a weasel, hungry as if
You hadn't had a decent meal in weeks,
Thundering in on a wave of rock and roll,
Your duffle-bag full of funky socks.

Toward dawn, reality
Slipping in on whiffs of coffee,
You added heft, subtracted hair, became
That thirty-plus man we never get news from.

Yeah, this is the usual whine for maternal access,
As if I'd never had those publications,
Was just some sink-bound whimperer, poor Mom.
Listen, kid; I get along fine without you.

We both remember that Viking-bearded boy
Took a few wounds, and scared the living beJesus
Out of the old folks more times than a few,
Trying on lots of stuff I had no time for,
Back in my slim days, tending you—
The firstborn wear the glow of pure potential,
Sweet as their birthbloom, and about as lasting.

So: how's it going? Good luck on those tests.

I keep sending sass and bruises, when I wish
I could send some charm: some sword, some healing magic,
That would call every bird of the sky down to your aid,

When you are lost and bruised and sore afraid.

I send what I have in the envelope of my years.
The taste of home-made bread fresh from the oven;
Wood smoke smells and chain saw whines and the nose tang
Of wet wool and freezing sheep shit,
And cut alfalfa curing in June sun.
The ticks and pops of wood heat, and soft laughter
Behind closed doors.
The rain clatter
Of the typewriter late at night.

LARGE BRASS KEY

Julie Gard

The purpose of life is creation; the purpose is my daughter. At any moment, one can interrupt the other. She bursts into the room while I'm writing; my mind drifts to a poem in the middle of her sentence. My daughter is real in the kitchen—I can hear her making a sandwich—but this page is real in my study, like the key she found on a side street off Nevsky. I told her it opened Russia. *Mom, stop,* she said, but she brought it home. Now we share this one thing comfortably, the key that's in her room and in my mind.

THE INEFFABLE *THING*

Patricia Barone

remembering my son's first words

The shape of your mouth, the way
your lips close and hum
then open for a burst
of exhaled breath—your first round *mahm.*

Summoning honey, your tongue
withdraws to your soft palate; your tone
vibrates through your nose
when you beg for *milk.*

How your tongue curls up
around *bird!*
Bees, a plosive puff,
buzz vibrations in your throat.

A fish zips out as you echo me—*fish!*
Then it is gone and you suspect
a sleight of my big hands.

Another goldfish swims beneath your nose,
and you say *thing!*—your tongue between your teeth—
thing! The shell-like word we humans use

to hold what our tongues cannot catch—
a shape alters light,
fleeting shadows whisk
around the corners of our minds.

Maybe a magician's trick,
a sort of thimblerig:
As if beneath three cups,
rocks, hats, or waving kelp,
you don't find the hidden thimble—

only azure feathers, gold-leaf flecks
of fin in rushing water.

Saying Our Names

Marianne Murphy Zarzana
                    for Judi Brown

Notice how just one syllable—
say *Jack*—can expand and become
the world, round and whole,
when it is a child's name
being formed by a mother's mouth.

I've overheard women in stores and airports,
restaurants and trains, sprinkling their talk
with the name of a brand new baby or
a grown child—*Morgen, Nora,
Michael, Kyle, Joseph, Ava-Rose.*

They sing each vowel and consonant
so the name stands out, resonates,
a pure bell whether the tone struck
is a major key, proud and strong,
or a diminished minor note.

Sometimes, when our daughter catches
her own name, *Elaine May,* part of a story
I am telling a sister over the phone,
later she'll ask, quasi-annoyed,
were you talking about me?

Yes, endlessly, shamelessly, I tell stories
about you. I say those fluid syllables,
chosen for the meaning—light—
and to honor your grandmothers,
chosen after discarding countless names.

Yes, I say them again and again and wonder
at the world they have become. Is this
how God says our names? Is this why sometimes
when I hear the wind rustling through the trees,
I turn and listen?

One Reason for Peace in an Infinite Universe

Carolyn Williams-Noren

Half a hard-boiled egg: choose an axis, slice.
Yolk obedient inside white.

Inside the apple, a star. Half a cup of water: harder—
it takes a container. Half a lake might take

years, but it can be done. A mathematician
says even infinity can be cut

in half: just divide by two. Any point

in an infinite field is the center. Exactly as much lies

in front of me as behind me. The planets, my bed,
other beds, my babies, dishes
done and not done, the sea grey house we live in
and women and men unseen. Our moon. Other
moons.

The poet on the radio says lie on the ground

and call the sky outward, not up. The earth
isn't under us; it's a thin wall at our backs.

Beyond my baby's face, this wall of earth.
Beyond the wall, maybe a dreamer on her back, eyes open, throat
open to the other half of everything, more stars rising.

CONTRIBUTORS

Catherine Barnett is the author of three poetry collections, *Into Perfect Spheres Such Holes Are Pierced* (2004), *The Game of Boxes* (2012), winner of the James Laughlin Award of the Academy of American Poets, and *Human Hours*, just published by Graywolf Press. She has received a Guggenheim Fellowship and a Whiting Award.

Patricia Barone has published her two most recent poetry collections, *Your Funny, Funny Face* and the *Scent of Water* with Blue Light Press. New Rivers Press published another collection, *Handmade Paper*, and *The Wind*, a novella. She describes herself as a Mississippi River writer.

Ellen Bass is the author of many poetry collections, including *Indigo* (2020), *Like a Beggar* (2014), *The Human Line* (2007), and *Mules of Love* (2002). Her poetry has frequently appeared in *The New Yorker* and *The American Poetry Review*. A Chancellor of the Academy of American Poets, she teaches in the MFA writing program at Pacific University.

Katie Bickham is the author of two collections of poems: *Mouths Open to Name Her* (LSU Press 2019) and *The Belle Mar* (Pleiades 2015), which won the Lena-Miles Wever Todd Poetry Prize. Katie has also won the Rattle Reader's Choice Award and the Missouri Review Editor's Prize. She teaches creative writing at Bossier Parish Community College in Louisiana.

Kris Bigalk has authored two poetry collections, *Enough* and *Repeat the Flesh in Numbers*, and has won two Minnesota State Arts Board grants in poetry. She founded and directs the creative writing program at Normandale Community College, and serves on the Board of Directors of the Association of Writers and Writing Programs.

Kimberly Blaeser is the author of four poetry collections—most recently *Copper Yearning* (2019), and editor of *Traces in Blood, Bone, and Stone: Contemporary Ojibwe Poetry*. She served as Wisconsin Poet Laureate for 2015-16. Blaeser, who is Anishinaabe, is a Professor at the University of Wisconsin—Milwaukee and MFA faculty member of the Institute of American Indian Arts in Santa Fe.

Adrian Blevins is the author of three full-length poetry collections: *Appalachians Run Amok*, *Live from the Homesick Jamboree*, and *The Brass Girl Brouhaha*. She is the recipient of many awards and honors including a Kate Tufts Discovery Award and a Rona Jaffe Foundation Writers' Award, among many others. She is a professor of English at Colby College in Waterville, Maine.

Emilie Buchwald, PhD, D.Hum.L., is author of *The Moment's Only Moment*, silver winner of the Benjamin Franklin Award, editor of three poetry anthologies, winner of the Lyric award, the author of four award-winning children's books, founding co-publisher (emeritus) of Milkweed Editions, founding Publisher of The Gryphon Press, and recipient, National Book Critics Circle Lifetime Achievement Award.

Cullen Bailey Burns is the author of two books of poetry, *Slip* and *Paper Boat,* both of which were finalists for Minnesota Book Awards. She now lives in Richmond, California and teaches at City College of San Francisco.

Paula Cisewski is author of *Quitter,* her fourth collection, which won the Diode Editions Book Prize. Her other books are *The Threatened Everything, Ghost Fargo* (selected by Franz Wright for the Nightboat Poetry Prize), *Upon Arrival,* and several chapbooks, including the lyric prose *Misplaced Sinister.* She lives in Minneapolis, where she teaches, collaborates with fellow artist-activists, and serves as an editor of *Conduit.*

Allison Adelle Hedge Coke, Distinguished Professor of Creative Writing UC Riverside, is the inaugural Excellent Foreign Poet / 1st Jade Sihui Female Poet Award, is a 2019 Fulbright Scholar, and the 2020 Dan & Maggie Distinguished Chair in Democratic Ideals for the University of Hawai'i. She has published six books of poetry, a memoir, a play, and ten anthologies.

Deborah Cooper is the author of five collections of poetry, most recently *Blue Window*, released in 2017 by Clover Valley Press. She is a retired Hospice Chaplain, living in Duluth, Minnesota. Deborah used poetry extensively in her hospice work, and has taught poetry in a variety of settings, in jails, juvenile centers and homeless shelters. Deborah is a former Duluth Poet Laureate.

Maryann Corbett is the author of four books of poems; a fifth is due out in 2020. Her third book, *Mid Evil,* won the Richard Wilbur Award for 2014, and her work is included in *The Best American Poetry 2018.* She is retired after thirty-five years of work for the Minnesota Legislature.

Barbara Crooker is a poetry editor for *Italian Americana*, and author of nine full-length books of poetry; *Some Glad Morning* (Pitt Poetry Series) is her latest. Her awards include the W.B. Yeats Society of New York Award, the Thomas Merton Poetry of the Sacred Award, and three Pennsylvania Council on the Arts Creative Writing Fellowships.

Sue Reed Crouse is a graduate of the Foreword Program, a two-year poetry apprenticeship at the Loft Literary Center in Minneapolis. She has presented her poetry and collage to grief groups, after losing her beloved daughter in 2008. Her work appears in many journals and has won awards. Her manuscript, *One Black Shoe*, was a finalist for the Backwaters Poetry Prize.

Heidi Czerwiec is the author of the lyric essay collection *Fluid States* and the poetry collection *Conjoining*, and is the editor of *North Dakota Is Everywhere: An Anthology of Contemporary North Dakota Poets*. She writes and teaches in Minneapolis, where she is an Editor for *Assay: A Journal of Nonfiction Studies*.

Florence Chard Dacey has published four poetry collections: *The Swoon, The Necklace, Maynard Went this Way,* and *Rock Worn by Water.* She is the recipient of seven regional arts council Artist Career Grants, a Loft-McKnight Award in poetry, and a Pablo Neruda Poetry Prize. She lives in Northfield, Minnesota.

Teri Ellen Cross Davis's poetry collection *Haint* (Gival Press) won the 2017 Ohioana Book Award for Poetry. Her work has appeared in many journals including *Poetry Ireland Review* and *Tin House*. She's a Cave Canem fellow, member of the Black Ladies Brunch Collective, and lives in Silver Spring, Maryland.

Alison Hawthorne Deming is the author most recently of the poetry collection *Stairway to Heaven* and the nonfiction book *Zoologies: On Animals & the Human Spirit*. She has been awarded a Guggenheim Fellowship, the Walt Whitman Award, and two National Endowment for the Arts Fellowships, among other honors. She is Regents Professor at the University of Arizona in Tucson.

Norita Dittberner-Jax has published five collections of poetry, most recently, *Crossing the Waters* (Nodin Press, 2017), which won the Midwest Book Award in Poetry. *Now I Live Among Old Trees* is forthcoming from Nodin Press. Norita has won awards for her work, including several nominations for the Pushcart Prize. A poetry editor for Red Bird Chapbooks, she lives in Saint Paul, Minnesota.

Carol Dorf has two chapbooks available, *Some Years Ask* (Moria Press), and *Theory Headed Dragon* (Finishing Line Press). Her poetry appears in *Bodega, E-ratio, Great Weather For Media, About Place, Glint, Slipstream, The Mom Egg, Sin Fronteras, The Journal of Humanistic Mathematics, Scientific American, Shofar,* and *Maintenant.* She is poetry editor of *Talking Writing* and teaches math in Berkeley, California.

Lorena Duarte is Salvadoran born, Minnesota raised, and Harvard educated. She is a poet, playwright, and performer and has received grants from the Jerome Foundation and the Minnesota State Arts Board. Her work has been published in anthologies such as *The Wandering Song: Central American Writing in the United States* (2017), and *Theatre Under My Skin: Contemporary Salvadoran Poetry* (2014).

Alice Duggan has had poems appear in *Tar River Poetry, Alaska Quarterly Review, Poetry East* and elsewhere; also in a chapbook, *A Brittle Thing*, and an anthology, *Home*, from Holy Cow! Press. She's interested in dailiness, plain speech, the timbre of voices, and telling stories.

Camille T. Dungy is a poet, essayist and editor whose books include *Trophic Cascade, Guidebook to Relative Strangers: Journeys into Race, Motherhood and History*, and *Black Nature: Four Centuries of African American Nature Poetry*. A 2019 Guggenheim Fellow, other honors include two NEA Fellowships, an American Book Award, and two NAACP Image Award nominations. Dungy is a professor at Colorado State University.

Iris Jamahl Dunkle is the author of three poetry collections, including *Interrupted Geographies* (2017). Her biography about Charmian Kittredge London, *Jack London's Wife*, will be published by the University of Oklahoma Press in 2020. She was the Poet Laureate of Sonoma County 2016-2018. She teaches at Napa Valley College and is the Poetry Director of the Napa Valley Writers' Conference.

Mary Moore Easter is a Pushcart Prize-nominated poet, Cave Canem Fellow, veteran dancer and choreographer, emerita professor of dance at Carleton College, and has two daughters and four grandchildren. Her debut collection, *The Body of the World* (Mad Hat Press 2018), was a finalist for the 2019 MN Book Award in Poetry.

Toni Easterson raises flowers at an organic farm in Minnesota. Her poetry has appeared in many publications, and when living in Connecticut, she was a regular Op Ed writer for the *Hartford Courant*. She recently received a Southeastern Minnesota Arts Council Grant for a series of work entitled "Pond Fauna."

Heid E. Erdrich is author of seven collections of poetry and a memoir-in-recipes. She edited *New Poets of Native Nations*. Her book *Little Big Bully* won a National Poetry Series award and will be published by Penguin in 2020. Heid is Ojibwe enrolled at Turtle Mountain.

Patricia Fargnoli is the author of five books and three chapbooks. Her latest, *Hallowed: New & Selected Poems* (Tupelo Press 2017) won the 2019 NH Literary Award for Outstanding Book of Poetry. The NH Poet Laureate from 2006-2009, her other awards include a MacDowell Fellowship, The May Swenson Book Award, The Sheila Motton Book award among others. She lives in Walpole, NH.

Jessi Marie Faue has been writing poetry since elementary school. She was first published as a sixth grade student in the *Anthology of Poetry for Young Americans.* Jessi is a registered nurse, army veteran, and the mother to three darling daughters. She is a local performance poet and currently helps facilitate Warrior Writers, a writing group for Veterans, in the Twin Cities.

Beth Ann Fennelly, the poet laureate of Mississippi, teaches in the MFA Program at the University of Mississippi, where she was named Outstanding Teacher of the Year. She's won grants from the N.E.A., United States Artists, and a Fulbright to Brazil. Her sixth book, *Heating & Cooling: 52 Micro-memoirs* (W. W. Norton) was an *Atlanta Journal Constitution* Best Book of 2018.

Jessica Fisher is the author of *Frail-Craft*, winner of the Yale Younger Poets Prize, and *Inmost*, awarded the Nightboat Poetry Prize. Her poems appear in such journals as *The American Poetry Review*, *The Believer*, *The Bennington Review*, *The New Yorker*, and *Tin House*. She received the Rome Prize in Literature, among many other fellowships, and teaches at Williams College.

Ann Fisher-Wirth is the author of *The Bones of Winter Birds* (Terrapin 2019) and *Mississippi*, a collaboration with photographer Maude Schuyler Clay (Wings 2018). Ann coedited *The Ecopoetry Anthology* (Trinity). Senior fellow of the Black Earth Institute, 2017 Poet in Residence at Randolph College, recipient of residencies at Djerassi, Hedgebrook, and elsewhere, Ann teaches at the University of Mississippi.

Carrie Fountain was born and raised in Mesilla, New Mexico, where her family's multicultural history is deeply rooted. Her first poetry collection, *Burn Lake*, was a National Poetry Series winner, which Penguin Random House published in 2010, followed by *Instant Winner* in 2014. Fountain also writes books for children and young adults. In 2019, Fountain was named Poet Laureate of Texas.

Rebecca Foust is the author of, among others, *The Unexploded Ordnance Bin* (Swan Scythe Press Award) and *Paradise Drive* (Press 53 Poetry Award), reviewed in the *Times Literary Supplement*. Recognitions include the James Hearst poetry prize and fellowships from Hedgebrook, MacDowell, and Sewanee. A former Marin County Poet Laureate, Foust edits poetry *Women's Voices for Change* and co-produces a Marin TV series, *Rising Voices*.

Julie Gard is author of the prose poetry collection *Home Studies* (New Rivers Press), which was a finalist for the 2016 Minnesota Book Award, and other publications including *Scrap: On Louise Nevelson* (Ravenna Press) and two chapbooks. A former Fulbright Graduate Fellow, she lives in Duluth, Minnesota, and is Associate Professor of Writing at the University of Wisconsin-Superior.

Jenn Givhan, an NEA and PEN/Rosenthal Emerging Voices fellowship recipient, is the author of four poetry collections, most recently *Rosa's Einstein* (Camino Del Sol Poetry Series), and the novel *Trinity Sight* (Blackstone Press). Her poems appeared in *Best of the Net*, *Best New Poets*, *Poetry Daily*, *Verse Daily*, *POETRY*, *The New Republic*, and *Kenyon Review*. She has received *New Ohio Review*'s Poetry Prize.

Arielle Greenberg is coauthor, with Rachel Zucker, of *Home/Birth: A Poemic*, and coeditor of four anthologies. Her most recent books are the poetry collection *Slice* (Coconut Books, 2015) and the creative nonfiction book *Locally Made Panties* (Ricochet Editions, 2016). Greenberg lives in Maine, where she teaches in the community and in the Oregon State University-Cascades' MFA program.

Sonia Greenfield is the author of two full-length collections: *Letdown*, selected for the Marie Alexander Series (February 2020, White Pine Press) and *Boy With a Halo at The Farmer's Market*, winner of the Codhill Poetry Award for 2014. Her chapbook, *American Parable*, won the 2017 Autumn House Press prize. She lives in Minneapolis and teaches at Normandale College.

Susan Griffin, essayist, poet, novelist, and playwright, has written twenty books, one a Pulitzer Prize finalist. Whether pairing ecology and gender in her foundational work, *Woman and Nature*, or the private life with the targeting of civilians, in *A Chorus of Stones*, she has explored countless contemporary issues, including climate change, war, colonialism, the body, democracy, and terrorism.

Hedy Habra has authored three poetry collections, including *The Taste of the Earth* (Press 53, 2019). *Tea in Heliopolis* won the USA Best Book Award and *Under Brushstrokes* was a finalist for the USA Best Book Award and the International Poetry Book Award. Her story collection, *Flying Carpets*, won the Arab American Book Award's Honorable Mention.

Margaret Hasse, author of *Between Us* (2016) and four other books of poems, is originally from Vermillion, South Dakota. Now living in St. Paul, Minnesota, she writes, teaches, and works on projects with arts organizations and other writers. She has received poetry fellowships from the National Endowment for the Arts, Minnesota State Arts Board, and The Loft-McKnight, among others.

Roberta Hill (Roberta Hill Whiteman), a Wisconsin Oneida, has published four collections of poetry, including *Star Quilt*, *Her Fierce Resistance*, *Philadelphia Flowers*, and *Cicadas: New and Selected Poems*. She has read her poetry internationally and is a Professor of English and American Indian Studies affiliated with the Nelson Institute for Environmental Studies at the University of Wisconsin-Madison.

Brenda Hillman is the author of ten books of poetry, including *Extra Hidden Life, among the Days (2018)*. With her mother Helen Hillman, she has translated the work of Ana Cristina Cesar. Hillman currently serves as a Chancellor for the Academy of American Poets and teaches at St. Mary's College of California.

JP Howard is the author of *say/mirror*, a Lambda Literary Award finalist, and *bury your love poems here*. She co-edited *Black Lesbians—We Are the Revolution!* for the journal *Sinister Wisdom*. A finalist for Split This Rock's Freedom Plow Award for Poetry & Activism, JP curates Women Writers in Bloom Poetry Salon and participates in Lambda Literary's LGBTQ Writers in Schools program.

Marie Howe was born in Rochester, New York. She worked as a newspaper reporter and teacher before receiving her MFA from Columbia University. She is the author of four award-winning books of poetry: *Magdalene*, *The Kingdom of Ordinary Time*, *What the Living Do*, and *The Good Thief*, which was selected by Margaret Atwood for the 1987 National Poetry Series.

Diane Jarvenpa is the author of five books of poetry, including *The Way She Told Her Story* (2018). She is a teaching artist with the Alzheimer's Poetry Project in Minneapolis and a singer/songwriter who records under the name Diane Jarvi.

Deborah Keenan is the author of ten collections of poetry, and a book of writing ideas, *from tiger to prayer*. Recently retired after 30 years as a professor in the MFA Program at Hamline University, she's the recipient of two Bush Foundation Fellowships and an NEA fellowship, and has been both a Loft Mentor participant and a Mentor. She lives by the river in beautiful, mysterious St. Paul, Minnesota.

Athena Kildegaard is the author of *Course, Ventriloquy,* and three other books of poetry. Her poems have been set to music by numerous composers. She teaches at the University of Minnesota Morris where she also directs the Honors Program.

Patricia Kirkpatrick has published *Blood Moon, Odessa,* winner of a Minnesota Book Award for Poetry, *Century's Road,* and picture books. Her awards include fellowships from the National Endowment for the Arts, The Loft, McKnight Foundation, and Minnesota State Arts Board. She has taught in many colleges and worked as an editor with well-known and emerging writers.

Kathryn Kysar is the author of two books of poetry, *Dark Lake* and *Pretend the World,* and she edited the anthology *Riding Shotgun: Women Write About Their Mothers.* She has received fellowships from the Minnesota State Arts Board, the National Endowment for the Humanities, and the Oberholtzer Foundation. She co-chairs the creative writing program at Anoka-Ramsey Community College.

Julie Landsman is author of three memoirs that capture the voices and stories of her students. Her first love, however, is poetry. Her poems have appeared in magazines and anthologies. She and poet George Ella Lyon founded the *I Am From Project* and encourage all to send poems to join the voices there. Julie teaches for the Alzheimer's Poetry Project.

Sherry Quan Lee, MFA, University of Minnesota, is the author of *Chinese Blackbird,* a memoir in verse; *Love Imagined: A Mixed Race Memoir;* plus *And You Can Love Me: a story for everyone who loves someone with Autism Spectrum Disorder,* a picture book. She is also the editor of *How Dare We! Write: A Multicultural Creative Writing Discourse* for university writing classrooms.

Sigi Leonhard is the author of the novel *Stimmen,* the chapbook *When You Fall Asleep,* and poems published in *Hunger Mountain, Absorb the Colors, A Rich Salt Place and Penchant.* Her play "Truth Serum" received a staged reading at the Minneapolis Playwrights Center in 2018. A professor at Carleton College, she has published scholarly work on German literature and film.

Layli Long Soldier is the author of *WHEREAS,* (Graywolf Press 2017), which won the National Book Critics Circle award and was a finalist for the National Book Award. She is the recipient of a 2015 Native Arts and Cultures Foundation National Artist Fellowship, a 2015 Lannan Literary Fellowship, and a 2016 Whiting Award. She lives in Santa Fe, New Mexico.

Jeanne Lutz grew up on a dairy farm, attended the National University of Ireland Galway, and spent two years in Japan. A Loft Mentor Series fellow for poetry, her work has appeared in *The Missouri Review, NonBinary Review, Conduit,* and elsewhere. She divides her time between the family farm and working at the Minneapolis Institute of Art.

Freya Manfred, a longtime Midwesterner who has also lived on both coasts, is the author of two memoirs and nine books of poetry. Her award-winning poems have appeared in over a hundred reviews and magazines and more than forty anthologies. Her work celebrates the vital lifeline of nature, our fragile mortality, humor, and the passionate arc of long-term relationships.

Jennifer Manthey has published poems in journals such as *Prairie Schooner, Calyx, Crab Orchard Review, Tinderbox Poetry Journal,* and *Best New Poets.* She has served as Assistant Poetry Editor for *Water~Stone Review,* and reads for *Palette Poetry Journal.* She teaches classes at the Loft Literary Center in Minneapolis and works in non-profit development.

Carol Masters is the author of *Dear Descendent,* poetry, published by Nodin Press, 2019. *You Can't Do That: Marv Davidov, Nonviolent Revolutionary,* was a finalist for the Midwest Independent Publishers Award in 2009. She is a mother, grandmother, and step-great grandmother.

Michelle Matthees has had poems in numerous journals, including *Memorious, Cleaver, The Prose Poem Project, J Journal, Superstition Review, Conduit,* and *Baltimore Review.* In 2016 New Rivers Press published her first book-length collection of poems, *Flucht.* She has received grants from the Minnesota State Arts Board, The Jerome Foundation, and other arts organizations. She lives in Duluth, Minnesota.

Jo McDougall is author of the recent poetry collections *The Undiscovered Room* (Tavern Books) and *In the Home of the Famous Dead: Collected Poems* (University of Arkansas Press). She is currently Poet Laureate of Arkansas and the 2019 recipient of the Porter Prize Lifetime Achievement Award. She lives in Little Rock.

Ethna McKiernan has received two Minnesota State Arts Board grants in poetry. Her first book, *Caravan,* was nominated for the Minnesota Book Award. In 2019, Salmon Poetry (Ireland) published *Swimming with Shadows.* McKiernan works in Street Outreach serving Minneapolis's homeless population. Formerly, she was the CEO of Irish Books and Media, Inc., a school-bus driver, and a grape-picker in France.

Leslie Adrienne Miller has published collections of poetry that include *Y*, *The Resurrection Trade,* and *Eat Quite Everything You See* from Graywolf Press, and *Yesterday Had a Man In It*, *Ungodliness*, and *Staying Up For Love* from Carnegie Mellon University Press. Professor of English at the University of St. Thomas, she holds degrees from the University of Missouri, Iowa Writers Workshop, and the University of Houston.

Rachel Morgan is the author of the chapbook *Honey & Blood, Blood & Honey* and co-editor of *Fire Under the Moon: An Anthology of Contemporary Slovene Poetry*. Her work recently appeared in the anthology *Fracture: Essays, Poems, and Stories on Fracking in America*. Currently she teaches at the University of Northern Iowa and is an Editor for the *North American Review*.

Rachel Moritz is the author of two books of poetry, *Borrowed Wave* (Kore Press, 2015) and *Sweet Velocity* (Lost Roads Press, 2017). She's also the co-editor of an essay collection, *My Caesarean: Twenty-One Mothers on the C-Section Experience and After* (The Experiment, 2019). She lives with her wife and son in Minneapolis.

Sanjana Nair, published in a wide range of journals, is deeply invested in both poetry and collaboration, taking part in Emotive Fruition, serving as the first treasurer for Kundiman and working with composers to write The Lady Apple, performed at NYC's Flea Theater and featured on NPR's Soundcheck. She's a full-time professor at CUNY's John Jay College of Criminal Justice.

Riki Kölbl Nelson, poet and artist, is co-founder of Penchant, formerly Northfield Women Poets. In addition to her contributions to the group's anthologies, she has published a bilingual collection of poems, *Borders/Grenzen* and a chapbook, *The Fall Heart*. She continues to write, exhibit her art, and to teach.

Naomi Shihab Nye was born to a Palestinian father and an American mother and began writing poems at the age of six. She is the Young People's Poet Laureate of the United States, 2019-2021, appointed by the Poetry Foundation. Her latest book is *The Tiny Journalist*.

Elizabeth Oness is a poet, fiction writer, and musician, who lives on a biodynamic farm in Southeast Minnesota. Her books include: *Articles of Faith*, *Departures*, *Twelve Rivers of the Body*, *Fallibility* and *Leaving Milan*. Elizabeth directs marketing and development for Sutton Hoo Press, a literary fine press, and is a professor of English at Winona State University.

Alicia Suskin Ostriker is a poet and critic who has written poems focused on pregnancy and motherhood—and many other topics—since 1964. Her best known collection on the actual and mythic experience of motherhood is *The Mother/Child Papers* (1980, reprinted 1986, 2008).

Sheila Packa writes about change and identity. She has four books, *The Mother Tongue, Echo & Lightning, Cloud Birds,* and *Night Train Red Dust: Poems of the Iron Range.* Recently her poems were set into a musical composition in *Sibelius: Kullervo & Kortekangas: Migrations* by the Minnesota Orchestra and recorded by BIS. Sheila was poet laureate of Duluth, Minnesota 2010-2012.

Linda Pastan is known for writing short poems that address topics like family life, domesticity, motherhood, the female experience, aging, death, loss and the fear of loss, as well as the fragility of life and relationships. Her most recent collections of poetry include *Insomnia, Traveling Light,* and *A Dog Runs Through It.*

Carol Kapaun Ratchenski is the author of two books of poetry, *A Beautiful Hell,* New Rivers Press, 2016, and *A Certain Kind of Forgiveness,* Meadowlark Press, 2019. Her work has won the Many Voices Project Award for poetry and the Birdy Poetry Prize. She lives in Fargo, North Dakota, where she is the owner/operator of the Center for Compassion and Creativity.

Katharine Rauk is the author of *Buried Choirs* (Tinderbox Editions) and the chapbook *Basil* (Black Lawrence Press). She currently teaches at North Hennepin Community College in Minnesota.

Paige Riehl is the author of the poetry collection *Suspension* (Terrapin Books, 2018) and the poetry chapbook *Blood Ties* (Finishing Line Press, 2014). She is the Poetry Editor for *Midway Journal,* a poetry mentor for the Minnesota Prison Writing Workshop, and an English faculty member at Anoka-Ramsey Community College.

Lia Rivamonte is the author of the poetry chapbook *Tell Me When You Get There.* She is the recipient of an Artist Initiative Grant from the Minnesota State Arts Board and a Metropolitan Regional Arts Council Next Step Grant. Rivamonte serves as a grants consultant for arts nonprofits in the Twin Cities.

Mary Kay Rummel has authored eight poetry books, recently *Cypher Garden.* Her books have won awards from New Rivers Press, Bright Hill Press and Blue Light Press. She is editor of *Psalms of Cinder & Silt,* poems about experiences with fires in California (Solo Novo Press).

A former poet laureate of Ventura County, California, she lives in Minneapolis and Ventura.

Edith Rylander has written poetry, memoir, and newspaper columns through a lifetime. *They've Packed up the Rock and Roll: Poems 1955-2018* (Red Dragonfly Press) is her most recent publication. She is twice a winner of a Bush Artists' Fellowship and a Loft-McKnight award, and has published widely in magazines and anthologies. She has three now-grown children.

Pamela Schmid is the creative nonfiction editor at *Sleet*, an online magazine, and the recipient of a 2013-14 Loft Mentor Series award. Her work has appeared in *Bellevue Literary Review, River Teeth, Baltimore Review, Blue Mesa Review, Sweet: A Literary Confection, Tahoma Literary Review* and elsewhere.

Julia Klatt Singer is the poet in residence at Grace Nursery School. She is co-author of *Twelve Branches: Stories from St. Paul,* (Coffee House Press), and author of four books of poetry. Her most recent, *Elemental* (Prolific Press) also has audio poems at OpenKim, as the element Sp. She's co-written songs with composers Craig Carnahan, Jocelyn Hagen, and Timothy Takach.

Joanna Solfrian is the author of *Visible Heavens,* chosen by Naomi Shihab Nye for a Wick First Book Prize, published by Kent State Press. Her poems have appeared in *The Harvard Review, Margie, The Southern Review, Pleiades, The Boston Review, Image,* and elsewhere. MadHat Press will publish her second collection, *The Mud Room,* in spring 2020.

Autumn Stephens is the author of the *Wild Women* book series and editor of two anthologies of women's first-person essays. The founder of an ongoing writing workshop for cancer survivors, she teaches generative and healing writing in the San Francisco Bay Area.

Joyce Sutphen is the author of more than eight volumes of poetry, including *Carrying Water to the Field* (2019). According to the Poetry Foundation, she is comfortable with traditional forms, and her poems often reference classic literary works. Her awards include The Barnard New Women Poets Prize, a Loft-McKnight Prize and a Minnesota Book Award.

Molly Sutton Kiefer, the author of *Nestuary,* a lyric essay, and three poetry chapbooks, has an MFA from the University of Minnesota. She runs Tinderbox Editions and is founding editor of *Tinderbox Poetry*

Journal. She lives with her family in Minnesota where she teaches English. Her work has appeared or is forthcoming in *Orion, Ecotone, The Rumpus,* among other publications.

Suzanne Swanson is the author of *House of Music* and the chapbook *What Other Worlds: Postpartum Poems.* She was awarded a place in the Loft Mentor Series and she helped to found Laurel Poetry Collective. A recently-retired perinatal psychologist, Suzanne is the mother of three. She rows on the Mississippi River and is happiest near big water.

Saymoukda Duangphouxay Vongsay is a Lao writer dead-set on amplifying refugee voices through experimental cultural productions. Smithsonian APAC and Theater Mu have presented her plays. Grants/ fellowships she's received include from Jerome Foundation, Knight Foundation, Playwrights' Center, The Loft Literary Center, Forecast Public Art, MRAC, and MSAB. Her picture book, *When Everything Was Everything,* celebrates former refugees and new Americans.

Claire Wahmanholm is the author of *Night Vision* (New Michigan Press, 2017), *Wilder* (Milkweed Editions, 2018), and *Redmouth* (Tinderbox Editions, 2019). Her poems have most recently appeared in, or are forthcoming from, *New Poetry from the Midwest* 2019, *Beloit Poetry Journal, Grist, RHINO, 32 Poems, West Branch,* and *The Southeast Review.* She lives and teaches in the Twin Cities.

Connie Wanek lived for over a quarter century in Duluth, Minnesota. Author of six books, Wanek was named a Witter Bynner Fellow of the Library of Congress. A children's book of poetry, co-written by Wanek and Ted Kooser, is forthcoming. In 2017 a wildflower trail in Duluth's Hartley Nature Center was named in her honor.

Wang Ping published 13 books of poetry and prose, including *Life of Miracles along the Yangtze and Mississippi, Of Flesh and Spirit, Aching for Beauty,* and *Ten Thousand Waves.* She's a recipient of NEA, Bush, Lannan and McKnight fellowships, founder and director of Kinship of Rivers project, and professor of English at Macalester College.

Karen Herseth Wee co-founded the still-active writing group Northfield Women Poets aka Penchant. She co-edited three of their four anthologies: *Absorb the Colors* (1984), *A Rich Salt Place* (1986), *Tremors Vibrations Enough to Change the World* (1995), and *Penchant* (2007). Personal publications include *Before Language* (chapbook, 1992), *The Book of Hearts* (a 1993 Minnesota Book Award finalist), and *Baksheesh, A Journey* (1994).

Kathleen Weihe is the author of a book of poetry, *Unless You Count Birds*. She recently retired from teaching English at Anoka-Ramsey Community College. She has received a Loft-McKnight Award, a fellowship from the Minnesota State Arts Board, and participated in the Loft's Mentor Series. She has an MFA from Hamline and lives with her family in Minneapolis, Minnesota.

Florence Weinberger is the author of five published collections of poetry, the most recent *Sacred Graffiti* and *Ghost Tattoo*. Four times nominated for a Pushcart Prize, her poetry has appeared in *The Comstock Review, Antietam Review, Rockvale Review, Nimrod, Poetry East, Rattle, Baltimore Review, Shenandoah, The River Styx, North American Review*, and others. Poems have also been published in numerous anthologies.

Miriam Weinstein holds a Bachelor of Arts degree from the University of Winnipeg and two Master of Education degrees from the University of Minnesota. Her chapbook, *Twenty Ways of Looking*, was published in 2017. Miriam's poetry appears in *Reflections on Home: The Heart of All That Is, Nuclear Impact: Broken Atoms in Our Hands, A Little Book of Abundance*, and several journals.

Elizabeth Weir lives in Minnesota. Her book of poetry, *High on Table Mountain*, was published by North Star Press of St. Cloud and was nominated for the 2017 Midwest Book Award. She received four Writer-to-Writer awards. Her work has been published in many journals, including *Evening Street Review, Water~Stone, Comstock Review, The Kerf* and *Holy Cow! Press* anthologies.

Gwen Nell Westerman is the author of *Follow the Blackbirds* (2013), a collection of poems in Dakota and English. Her poetry is also included in the 2018 anthology *New Poets of Native Nations*. A member of the Sisseton Wahpeton Oyate, she teaches English and Humanities at Minnesota State University, Mankato.

Lesley Wheeler is the author of nine books, including the poetry collection *The State She's In* and the forthcoming novel *Unbecoming*. Poetry Editor of *Shenandoah* and winner of fellowships from Fulbright and the National Endowment for the Humanities, she lives in Virginia.

Zoë Ryder White has poems that have appeared in *Thrush, Hobart, Sixth Finch, Threepenny Review, Crab Creek Review*, and *Subtropics*, among others. She co-authored a chapbook, *A Study in Spring*, with Nicole Callihan. A former public elementary school teacher, she edits books for educators about the craft of teaching.

Carolyn Williams-Noren has poems that can be found in *AGNI*, *Cimarron Review*, *Sweet*, and other journals, and in two chapbooks: *Small Like a Tooth* (Dancing Girl Press, 2014) and *FLIGHTS* (Ethel, 2020). Her lyric essay about early motherhood, published in *Willow Springs* in summer 2017, was named on the "Notable Essays" list in *Best American Essays 2018*.

Kao Kalia Yang wrote two award-winning memoirs, *The Latehomecomer* and *The Song Poet*. Recently she debuted a children's book, *A Map Into the World*, and co-edited collection, *What God is Honored Here?* Her children's book, *The Shared Room*, and collective memoir of refugee stories, *Somewhere in the Unknown World*, will be published in 2020.

Ye Chun is the author of two books of poetry, *Lantern Puzzle* and *Travel over Water*, a novel in Chinese, and two books of translations, *Ripened Wheat: Selected Poems of Hai Zi* and *Long River: Poems by Yang Jian* (co-translator). A recipient of an NEA fellowship and three Pushcart Prizes, she teaches at Providence College in Rhode Island.

Amy Young is a former poet laureate of Alexandria, Virginia, and is a teaching artist at The Lab School of Washington. Her work has been set to music and performed at the Smithsonian American Art Museum as well as at the Pittsburgh New Music Festival. Her poems have most recently been anthologized in *Ghost Fishing: An Eco-Justice Poetry Anthology*.

Tracy Youngblom has published two chapbooks of poems, *Driving to Heaven* (2010) and *One Bird a Day* (2018), as well as one full-length poetry collection, *Growing Big* (2013). Her individual poems, stories, and essays have been published in journals such as *Shenandoah, Briar Cliff Review, North Stone Review, New York Quarterly, Big Muddy, Wallace Stevens Journal, Dogwood, Ruminate, St. Katherine Review*, and other places.

Marianne Murphy Zarzana, a retired professor of English, Southwest Minnesota State University, Marshall, lives in Mishawaka, Indiana with her husband. Her poems have appeared in *Poetry of Presence: An Anthology of Mindfulness Poems, Stoneboat, Pasque Petals, Boomer Lit Mag, Dust & Fire, Umbrella Journal, Blue Earth Review*, and other journals.

CREDITS

Catherine Barnett, "Summons" from *Human Hours*. Copyright © 2018 by Catherine Barnett. Used by permission of The Permissions Company, LLC on behalf of Graywolf Press, Minneapolis, Minnesota.

Patricia Barone, "The Ineffable *Thing*" from *The Scent of Water*, Blue Light Press. Copyright © 2013 by Patricia Barone. Used by permission of the author.

Ellen Bass, "Cold" from *Like a Beggar*. Copyright © 2014 by Ellen Bass. Used by permission of The Permissions Company LLC on behalf of Copper Canyon Press.

Katie Bickham, "At Last, She Is Finished with Emptiness" from *Mouths Open to Name Her: Poems*, Louisiana State University Press. Copyright © 2019 by Katie Bickham. Used by permission of Louisiana State University Press.

Kris Bigalk, "Aren, Two Years Old, Playing at Orchard Park" from *Silk Road*. Copyright © 2012 by Kris Bigalk. Used by permission of the author.

Kimberly Blaeser, "Lost Mothers" and "On Climbing Petroglyphs." Copyright © 2020 by Kimberly Blaeser. Used by permission of the author.

Adrian Blevins, "Firstborn" from *Live from the Homesick Jamboree*, Wesleyan University Press. Copyright © 2009 by Adrian Blevins. Used by permission of Wesleyan University Press.

Adrian Blevins, "Still Life with Peeved Madonna" from *The Brass Girl Brouhaha*, Copper Canyon Press. Copyright © 2003 by Adrian Blevins. Used by permission of The Permissions Company LLC on behalf of Copper Canyon Press.

Emilie Buchwald, "Yes" from *The Moment's Only Moment*, Nodin Press. Copyright © 2018 by Emilie Buchwald. Used by permission of the author.

Cullen Bailey Burns, "We Just Want It To Be Healthy" from *Rattle*, Rattle Foundation. Copyright © 2006 by Cullen Bailey Burns. Used by permission of the author.

Paula Cisewski, "Empty Next Syndrome" from *The Threatened Everything*, Burnside Review Books. Copyright © 2017 by Paula Cisewski. Used by permission of the author.

Paula Cisewski, "Beloved Math" from *Ghost Fargo*, Nightboat Books. Copyright © 2010 by Paula Cisewski. Used by permission of the author.